Two Strokes Not Out

A Personal Experience Guide
for Stroke Survivors and their Families

SAS FREEMAN

Contents

Author Notes:

If all readers of this book benefit I have achieved my goal, if just a few stroke survivors receive help sooner rather than later, then my efforts recounting my journey and the hurdles along the way are both worthwhile and rewarded.

My book does not touch on anything medical; it doesn't intend to give advice – we have doctors, nurses, and physiotherapists etc. to do all that. I write simply from the patient's point of view, from my own experiences and feelings in the hope that they will be of help to you and your family. I wish you a full recovery.

I live in the UK and I am British so I have written primarily for the British reader hoping that my American readers will find it easy to follow and understand the main, very sincere message.

Dedication

To Nick and Henry for adapting to the new, scary situation we found ourselves suddenly thrown into and in loving memory of Ego, my friend and companion, there is no love like a dog's love.

FOREWORD

Anyone who has recently undergone treatment for a serious medical or surgical condition cannot fail to be amazed by the technical wizardry available in today's NHS. Joint replacement, keyhole surgery and minimally invasive treatments for serious heart disease are now commonplace. It is now a political and clinical given that this therapeutic revolution returns people to 'normal life' more quickly and effectively than in bygone days.

As a Urological Surgeon, I led a multidisciplinary team that included specialist nurses, physios and occupational therapists who provided the necessary information and backup to patients returning home so that they could resume normal life as painlessly as possible. Or so I thought until I found myself on the other side of the fence. It came as something of a shock to me as the husband of someone who had recently undergone major surgery to realise that all the available expertise fell short of the necessary backup to cope with daily living in the real world.

Stroke management has changed out of all recognition in the 40 years since I was a junior hospital doctor. In those days, active treatment and rehabilitation were rudimentary. Today, specialist stroke units treat stroke aggressively, and rehab and home assessment are an essential part of ongoing treatment. Nevertheless, many stroke patients will still leave hospital feeling as if they are trying to circumnavigate the globe without a compass, much less a satnav.

Suffering a stroke is not only a terrifying but also a profoundly life changing experience. Only a stroke sufferer could write such a book as this with this level of insight. This book will provide help, reassurance and guidance to stroke sufferers and their families and carers enabling them to feel reassured that there is a path to return to acceptably normal life. It is also a must-read for all healthcare professionals. As a wise old physician once told me, diabetics understand their condition much better than I do.

Malcolm Jones, Urological Surgeon [Retired].

Introduction

'I failed my way to success.'
Thomas Edison

Every year in the UK 150,000 people have a stroke – one person every five minutes. The majority of these are over 65, but it can happen at any age, even to babies. With our life-patterns changing, more and more young people are suffering strokes; the last figures show 1000 a year to people under the age of 30. I'm not sure of the figures for people under 55 but it's over 10,000.

The main thing is that there are many who survive and YOU are one of those survivors.

Stroke is the third largest killer but, with greater awareness and a few changes to our daily lives, up to 80 % of strokes could be prevented.

I wrote my book to help you identify and understand what you are feeling and facing at the moment and show you that, although it is tough and there will be tears and days when you just feel like giving up, there is light at the end of the tunnel and you can do it.

You can recover.

The three most important tools I held were:

- A positive mental attitude.
- The belief that I would make a full recovery.
- A sense of humour.

I realise that at this stage 'a sense of humour' sounds difficult but it is powerful. The ability to laugh at these alien limbs can help. They are attached to you but do not assist you in any shape or form, but trip you up and temporarily don't respond to your brain. What has happened to the days when they worked with you?

I should also mention how you mourn for the lifestyle and different roles you had, in my case my role as a partner, mother and joint provider. Your family also mourns and has to adapt to sudden changes and adjustments with extra work and responsibility forced upon them. The change can be a reversal with the child becoming the carer.

Who Am I?

It was suggested that you may appreciate knowing something about me and my life before I had a stroke and that seems to make sense.

I was 45 and mother of one. I was working and very often this took me away from home. I didn't do anything very clever but it involved a lot of driving and being flexible and able to juggle everything at the drop of a hat. Often work was announced suddenly with just hours to arrange the work and the drive, not to mention family needing to be sorted! Food, lifts to and from school, etc.

I had previously worked for an employer in advertising, who also owned a national leaflet company. He offered me work supervising teams distributing leaflets for national advertisers all over the country. This meant a great deal of travelling and staying away from home for long periods.

I also did modelling work, television and film/television extra work so, as you can see, the hours could be long and travel was countrywide. Sometimes I would come off air in the early hours of the morning and then be back at 7 a.m. for a full session before driving for several hours to another job. I spent many nights in hotel rooms.

I had just returned from Cornwall when I had my stroke. I was very fortunate to have returned home and not be in a hotel room, alone; or worse still driving.

I have always been naturally slim so I didn't have any reason to question my cholesterol level; I was active and fit. I practised yoga and Pilates, I went swimming every week, walked regularly and rode ex-racehorses, so I had plenty of fresh air and exercise.

I live with my partner, Nick, my son, Henry, and our whippet, Ego – not your everyday name for a dog but it's a long story and she chose us. I will save you that tale though!

I hope this will give you an image in your mind as I continue to share my experiences up till now rather than leaving you wondering who I am.

Chapter One

My Experience – The First 48 Hours

*'Little minds are tamed and subdued by misfortunes
but great minds rise above them'*
Washington Irving

There you are, living life as normal when suddenly you are hit by a strong pain in your head like nothing you have ever experienced before. Your whole life, as you knew it, along with your body are about to change around you; you are simply a bystander to what is happening. Everything has now been taken out of your control.

I had such a strong pain in my head but in a small area. I thought, 'It isn't a migraine because it isn't in the whole of my head but the pain is incredible, like nothing I've had before'. I lay down. Later I took some painkillers but they didn't help. I thought, 'They will work, they have to, I have to get to work but I'll be late because this is really bad and I have to drive a long way'.

My dog, who never barks, would not settle. 'Why, does she have to pick today of all days to act so out of character? I must get dressed and go to work and this will all wear off'.

I felt sick, my mouth and eye felt strange. Still I tried to get ready. I stumbled and fell a couple of times yet I did not question why. My dog was really annoying me now. I thought I heard a little voice saying, 'If you were older, I

13

would say you were having a stroke'. Then, 'Don't be silly, get ready for work'. My arm felt strange. I fell over again. My limbs felt heavy, odd as if I were a little drunk, out of control.

I tried to tell myself that my dog had tripped me up, she was being silly today. I wanted to sleep; I felt an inner calm and peace but then suddenly thought, 'I mustn't sleep, it's dangerous to sleep'. An inner voice said, 'You are having a stroke, you know that'. Yet, at the same time, I felt calm as if I was going to be all right. Nothing was making any sense so how could I be calm?

My eye was crying.

By this time I knew I needed help. I phoned my old doctor's surgery. I was on the phone but it felt as though I was tripping over my mouth, I couldn't get the words out. The receptionist offered me an appointment in a couple of days. I requested a call back and put the phone down. I lay down and felt fine, at peace. 'I will just sleep here. That's fine'. Then suddenly I panicked and the inner voice returned telling me to get help now. I was on the phone again. I explained my numb face, stumbling, struggling at this point to manage complete words. I still had the same response. I fell down and my speech was laboured and faltering. I think I managed to say, 'I need help now' and asked if I should call an ambulance but I was crying. The receptionist then said, 'If you can get here now you can be seen'.

The next bit I'm not proud of. I do not remember locking the house, driving this journey, locking the car or even where I left the car or how I got into the doctors, but I got there.

14

My 'stroke of luck' was the message telling me to just go and get there before I could not. Yet, at the same time as I knew I was going to be all right I suddenly felt worried about absolutely nothing. I had forgotten about work and the people who were waiting for me. All the things that go through our minds that we worry about on a daily basis had been erased; I was just there yet not thinking. Not worrying. It was pure bliss.

My car is an automatic and I now think that I must have used my left foot with one hand on the wheel as it's the only possible way I could have driven; in my right mind I would never have attempted such a thing. I only share this because it highlights my stupidity and the importance of phoning emergency services immediately, part of the reason for writing this book.

These first emotions are very different for everyone. For me it was a state of total blissfulness followed by total disbelief. 'No, not me, I'm too young'. How wrong and naïve was I? As I've mentioned, a stroke can strike anyone, even babies.

I continued thinking, 'No, it's not that, it can't be'. Then the reality hits. You are suddenly locked in your own bizarre world of frustration, inside your body which is behaving strangely with limbs you don't know anymore and which are letting you down. Your mind has words in it but, try as you might, they will not pass your lips with any type of sound that either you or anyone else can translate.

This is where my luck appeared to change. The doctor who saw me knew immediately what was wrong. I would like to thank her but sadly, I would not be able to recognise her as I was in such a state at the time. She contacted a colleague at the hospital and made sure that I would be met in Medical Assessment so that I would already be booked in and seen. I remember thinking I didn't want Nick or Henry to worry especially as Henry was playing rugby so, better to say I'm fine and just need to go to hospital. In hindsight this was probably worse but logic had left me hours earlier. I just did not want Henry worrying, then injured on the rugby field; and after all I was still too young to be having a stroke and this wasn't happening to me.

We are told that the damaged part of the brain is now dead, as it dies off during the attack causing the after effects. But, apart from the muscle and ligaments going into spasm, twisting and causing tightness or stiffness, there is no fundamental damage to the limbs. They are not broken in any way; it is simply a temporary breakdown of communication. It is a matter of reconnecting that circuit in the brain that tells the limbs how to function. If we hold on to these thoughts throughout our recovery they will help us.

From what I can recollect, my first night was spent in Medical Assessment having scans to ascertain whether I had suffered a bleed or a clot. I really can't remember going onto the Stroke Ward or my first few days there. It was almost as though things were happening and I was a distant observer vaguely paying attention. I had lost understanding of everything including myself. I could no longer communicate as my limbs on one side were completely alien. I was just lost in my own body, unable to make sense of anything, far too tired to really question yet at the same time somehow calm. It was completely bizarre.

The staff and doctors were all so kind and attentive, doing everything for me, explaining things which I neither understood nor remembered. They made me as comfortable as possible allowing me to have my own duvet as I always feel the cold. My friend, Sabine, brought in some artificial flowers to cheer the place up; they were so realistic they worked wonders. Others brought me some magazines so I had things to glance at as I began to feel able, albeit weeks later. I was there for two weeks before going in to Rehabilitation.

Things to remember:

- get help as soon as possible
- accept that denial is part of the recovery process
- family members: bring photographs of happy occasions and places for you to have by your bed

Chapter Two

Stroke – What Is It?

'What would life be like if we had no courage to attempt anything?'
Vincent Van Gogh

Stroke is a brain injury caused either by a bleed or a clot. I believe if you speak to a stroke patient each will remember the onset of their attack clearly, even if they didn't understand what was happening at the time. I can remember mine very vividly. One minute I was fine then the next I felt a sudden bolt of pain in just one small area on the left side of my head followed by a strange, heavy sensation in my arm and leg and unwillingness for them to behave as I wished. My mouth was dribbling and my face felt odd. Yet I did not put all the pieces together because I was convinced I was too young. Talking to other people later on in Rehab, they also recalled each detail right down to what was on television, until they eventually had help, in many cases only because someone visited. This is like a little time capsule in the memory bank with blanks on either side.

Stroke happens when the blood supply to part of the brain is reduced or cut off. Brain cells then become damaged or die because of the lack of oxygen and nutrients normally carried to them in the blood. A stroke is sudden and has immediate effects on the body but, remember, with hard work they can be reversed and we can recover.

The most common type of stroke, which I along with 80% of people have, is caused by a clot and called an **ischaemic stroke.** The other type which affects 20% is a bleed called a **haemorrhagic stroke;** this is when a blood vessel bursts within the brain or a subarachnoid haemorrhage when a blood vessel on the surface of the brain bleeds into the area between the brain and the skull.

The right half of the brain controls the left side of the body and vice versa. Talking, reading, writing and communicating are controlled by the left side of the brain; the right side is responsible for what we see, hear and touch and judge speed, distance, size, etc. Both control the movement of our limbs on the opposite side. It is very complex and the right and left functions are not always this distinct. Both hemispheres contribute to all processes but some more dominant in each side. The actual location of the clot or bleed can mean that all your senses are affected or, if you are fortunate, they are not.

I lost my sense of smell, had reduced and blurred sight in my right eye and hearing in my right ear. But, although the clot was on the side responsible for speech I only lost that during the early stages of the attacks and I now have difficulty just when I am tired or nervous in company.

Mini-Strokes – Transient Ischaemic Attack

This happens when the brain's blood supply is interrupted for a very short time and the brain is starved of oxygen. The symptoms are similar to a stroke but are temporary, lasting for only a few minutes or maybe a few hours. They disappear totally within 24 hours. You should not ignore the symptoms as they could be a sign that you may be at risk of having a stroke in the future, so do visit your doctor.

What can we do to reduce the risk of stroke in other family members and friends?

Smoking – If you can, give up or at least cut down. Smoking causes high blood pressure; chemicals are absorbed into the body and blood vessels are damaged. As a non-smoker I run the risk of sounding a bore here mentioning 'that same old chestnut' again but it is a fact that smoking causes strokes. It is one of the biggest causes of illnesses leading to premature death in the UK. There, lesson over! But seriously, nicotine and tobacco smoke contain over 4000 toxic chemicals which are deposited into the lungs then absorbed into the bloodstream. Some of these damage the walls of blood vessels resulting in furring and narrowing of the arteries; this increases the chances of a blood clot forming in the arteries to the heart and brain. It is said that people who smoke are three times more likely to have a stroke than non-smokers. Your local stroke unit will advise on smoking cessation programmes.

Blood pressure – Have it monitored; high blood pressure is a major cause.

Diabetes – This could put you at greater risk so ask your doctor for advice on other things you can do to help yourself.

Diet – A diet high in salt and fat is putting you at more risk by probably increasing your cholesterol. Try and eat more fruit and vegetables. I suggest you ask your doctor if you can have a cholesterol test. I am not overweight and love my chocolate, ice cream, cake and alcohol but I have lots of fresh vegetables, salad and fruit every day so I believed I ate healthily. I do not eat butter or spreads but have lots of cheese believing that calcium is good for me; I had no idea that I had a high cholesterol level.

Exercise – This is invaluable and can be fun. It's also something you can do as a family. Next time you go to your local pub, if it's possible, think of walking or cycling instead of driving. Small changes can make a difference. Lack of exercise can lead to a furring of the arteries. Exercise can help decrease blood pressure.

Oral contraceptives and Hormone Replacement Therapy – These are considered to have a slight risk factor but nothing is proven yet.

Migraine in women – It has been proved that women suffering from certain types of migraines are three times more likely to have an ischemic stroke.

Atrial Fibrillation (AF) – Most people are not even aware that they have this irregular heartbeat or that it can lead to a stroke. Some people may sense that their heart is beating quickly, are tired, have chest pains or breathlessness but others may have none of these symptoms. This is why it is so important that we ask our G.P's to check our blood pressure. A normal pulse rate should be between 60 and 100 beats per minute. If you suffer from AF your heart beat could be up to 140 per minute. This is far more common in older people but can affect people of any age. If diagnosed, you can be prescribed medication to prevent the risk of strokes.

Regular heavy drinking – This can raise blood pressure which increases the risk of strokes.

Recreational drugs – Amphetamines, ecstasy and cocaine can increase the risk of strokes especially in people with Arteriovenous Malfunctions (AVMs) –These occur when the structure of the arteries and veins is abnormal and gets tangled. People can have this condition yet be unaware until something goes wrong. If such a person's blood pressure is too high the more fragile veins and arteries can rupture leading to bleeding in the brain.

Ethnic background – Asians and African Caribbeans are at greater risk of a stroke than people from other ethnic groups. This is possibly because high blood pressure, diabetes and sickle cell diseases are more common in those particular groups.

Carotid artery disease – The two large arteries at the front of the neck are called carotid arteries and they carry the majority of the blood to the brain. Fatty material, called plaque, can build up in these which narrows and hardens them making it difficult for the blood to flow through – this is called atherosclerosis. This plaque can also attract blood clots causing blockages in the arteries making them even narrower – this is called carotid artery disease. If a clot gets dislodged in the brain it can cause a TIA (Transient Ischaemic Attack) or stroke. It is important to identify this condition since it is a warning sign of a potential stroke.

Common Problems after Stroke

During the first few weeks after a stroke the most difficult thing is trying to accept what has happened to you and how your whole life has changed overnight. Once you're out the other side of the denial stage, some of the things to deal with are weakness in limbs or total/partial paralysis (hemiplegia). This is one of the most common symptoms of a stroke. Looking around both Stroke Ward and Rehab, I don't remember anyone who was not affected by this. This can also be coupled with stiffness of the muscles and joints. I had tightness and pain in my hip joint and stiffness but no pain in my shoulder which was also slightly lowered.

Balance – Again, if my memory isn't playing tricks on me, I don't think there was anyone this missed out either. We were all making our way to and from our physio sessions looking as if we were heavily under the influence of alcohol, in my case longing for just one chilled glass of champagne to celebrate my improvements and to break the monotony of hospital water.

Swallowing – I was fortunate not to be affected by difficulties in swallowing. I have been able to eat and drink normally all the way through my recovery. However, it does affect about 50% of stroke patients and is called **dysphagia**. It can be dangerous if food goes down the wrong way so patients have to be helped with feeding or be given liquid feeds.

Dysgeusia – When your ability to taste is affected. I have experienced this slightly and even now add salt and sauces which I wouldn't have done before. This can cause food to taste strange or horrid or just reduce the sense of taste which is why you may add extra seasoning sometimes insulting people who have slaved for hours creating a supper dish you simply can't taste as others can.

Proprioception – This is something I have difficulty with. It tends to occur on your affected side. It is when the brain isn't aware of where your limbs are in space either with your eyes open or closed. One way to improve this is to put weight through your hands on a table or on the arms of a chair as often as possible. I try to do this every time I get up from a table or a chair with arms.

Dyspraxia – The inability to plan your movements accurately. You may lift your leg up to take a step but your foot seems to have a mind of its own and land down where it chooses and at any angle. This is something most of us struggle with.

Sleep and Tiredness – Some of the other patients on my ward had difficulty sleeping yet felt the same tiredness as me; this is not at all uncommon in stroke patients and very frustrating. I was able to sleep almost all the time. I ate breakfast and, exhausted by that, slept again, ate lunch and slept again and so on. I could still sleep all night. As I got stronger and had my physio sessions at home with the Intermediate Care Team (ICT) I slept between their treatments and after they left. Sleep is such a valuable source of recovery.

Dysphasia – Difficulties with speech.

Aphasia – absence of speech. This is most common in left-sided stroke damage. But some left-handed people have the language area of their brain in the right side. When people are affected in this way it is particularly frustrating because their thoughts are still active; they know what they want to communicate but are unable to. They are often unable to write so can't put their thoughts down on paper. They are temporarily locked in their own world, unable to communicate anything, sometimes referred to as 'locked in syndrome'. There are two types of aphasia. One is where the patient can understand what you are saying but can't talk back; the other is when they are also unable to comprehend either.

Eyesight – This is affected in many ways. In my case I had blurred vision and felt pressure in one eye. I couldn't enjoy reading because of the discomfort. It can also cause double vision or loss of part of the field of vision or complete loss of vision in one or both eyes. Some people display what seems to be odd behaviour by washing only part of their face or men only shaving a section. Some only eat food from one side of the plate. Reduced central vision is known as a visual processing problem when what the eye is seeing is not understood by the brain. This is particularly noticeable when coming in from bright sunshine as it takes the eye much longer to adjust to the change in light and you can't see. I was told that the muscles behind the eye become disabled but there are eye exercises to strengthen them, just as is done with limbs. One exercise is to concentrate on a line of dots on a piece of card trying to get them into focus.

Mental changes – The biggest and most noticeable changes for me were concentration and the processing of information, but they both returned, gradually. I also found it difficult to remember things. Someone would tell me what I was to do tomorrow but shortly afterwards I'd forgotten. It can be difficult to pay attention. By the time the person has finished the sentence you have forgotten the first part and can't grasp the whole content. It can also be difficult to make a simple decision. I remember my first cooking session with Headway who are a charitable organisation in the UK set up to help people with brain injuries. They were helping me try to plan the week's menu for Nick, Henry and me. I had improved a great deal at this stage so getting to do meals was to be another big step forward. But, although it used to be something I wouldn't think twice about before, just couldn't for the life of me think what we used to eat or what I could make. For the past six months I hadn't had to think of shopping or cooking; Nick had done all of that and I had just enjoyed what he'd put in front of me. I could not even remember what was available in the shops. As a double exercise they took me to a supermarket to remind myself and to give me confidence in going out.

Bladder and bowels – Some people have problems with incontinence but I am told that control is usually regained in a few weeks. Most patients suffer from constipation due to inactivity but that is easily remedied.

Mood swings – Emotions are all over the place after a stroke as your whole life has been turned upside down and you're trying to deal with the aftermath. Sometimes you feel sadness, depression, anger, anxiety and a loss of confidence but you are not on your own. We have all experienced these in varying degrees and they are all part of the recovery stage but they are difficult for the carer to cope with. They see the person they love now also having to battle with these ever-changing emotions seeming to be doing well and then suddenly bursting into tears. The carer can't ease or prevent this and sometimes may even be in the firing line themselves.

Personality – This may have changed after a stroke. Some people become aggressive and swear a lot; some appear to have little or no emotion; some may be very emotional crying at films that would never have affected them before.

Sensation – Some people are very sensitive to light, sound and colour or they may not feel sensations like heat or sharpness of objects. I spilt boiling water over my hand and didn't feel it; it blistered and needed dressing every day for some time yet still I didn't experience any sensation of burn-related pain.

What is the likelihood of having another stroke?

This is probably the biggest question stroke survivors ask themselves alongside the obvious one of, 'will I or when will I get better?' It is a question that is often asked subconsciously but not very often voiced for fear of the answer. Maybe it is something which should be discussed in the hospital with both family and patient as, after all, openness is the kindest option. Perhaps it may also be best before leaving hospital because otherwise the carer may assume that medication would prevent another stroke. I am sure that Nick won't mind me mentioning that this was definitely what he believed which is why, when I had my second stroke, his reaction was 'No, it's not because of her medication'. No one had taken the time to explain to him the realities of having a second stroke, a prime example of it being kinder to be forewarned.

'Forewarned is forearmed'.

About 10% of people have a second stroke most likely within the first twelve months. After a year the likelihood can lower to 5% but, remember we have all been put on relevant medication to reduce this risk, yet it is up to us to do our bit by making the appropriate changes I mentioned earlier – diet, smoking, exercise, etc.

Making Home Videos/CDs

This is something my friend and physio said we should have done but we didn't realise this until I was a long way into my journey. I strongly suggest you do this. I know your first reaction will be, 'Why do I want photographs of me at the moment when I am struggling and feel so vulnerable?' Believe me, you will be so pleased that you took them. This has been substantiated by an e-mail from a friend of mine in New

Zealand, a fellow stroke survivor, whose physiotherapist did exactly that. Paul told me how helpful it had been for him. 'I ask you to think hard: Is there really a reason **not** to do this? The help it will give you along your journey outweigh those reasons you have just aired and remember I would have used those very same ones but I see that the benefits are stronger. On the days when you don't feel you are making much progress a friend can pop on your video and reveal how much progress you've made just in the past two weeks or so'.

I found that I am so focused on my goals all the time that I forget what I've achieved. It is only when a nurse comes in who hasn't seen you for a while and says, 'Wow, look at that! Your foot isn't so turned' or 'You're moving another finger'. It can be anything but for someone to notice and comment, that's wonderful. But, if you have the same therapist they may be too familiar to notice all the small changes and, as time goes on, the changes become smaller. I found I made the most progress during the first three or four months and after that each bit was comparatively small. I also found that my arm and leg were much the same for ages and then suddenly my leg improved at a greater speed than my arm. It seems logical when we realise that with rehab we try and do extra little things ourselves like getting up to go to the toilet or make a drink so we are moving limbs even when we are not consciously doing physiotherapy.

Within your visual record make reference to all your firsts such as when you first made your sandwich for lunch, got out of a chair unaided or made your first drink; these are all huge milestones in our strange new world. You can also use home videos to analyse where you are going wrong or see where you need to make changes in quality not quantity. You may have speeded up your movements but have you lost some of their quality in doing so? So these need to be addressed before you get into bad habits.

When you look at your videos ask yourself some questions:
Do I look to be in danger when I move?
Are my movements more coordinated?

This is valuable to your progress as well as being a pick-me-up. Other people can see how we are improving so why shouldn't we have a look every now and then and give ourselves a pat on the back? You can also study your progress and note ways in which you can improve. Think of jockeys and trainers; they will study a race, analyse it and see how they can improve in the next race. Think of yourself as fine-tuning your recovery programme. This can also be used to help you in recovering your speech but some people find it more beneficial to just listen to their voice rather than watch the movement of their mouth so, try both video and audio and see which is most beneficial for you.

Remember that not only are you making a record to show how much progress you have made but you are also comparing *how* you are moving so make sure you are doing the exercises in the same place when you make the videos at roughly the same time of day. This may sound obvious but, as you know, the slightest difference in the height of a step, for instance, or an uneven surface or you are feeling tired will make a difference and you won't be making a true comparison. Ask the person who is making each video with you to record the date and time. You can buy video recorders quite cheaply nowadays and most mobile phones have built-in videos; you can then transfer your videos to your computer and view them that way.

Also do a storyboard. Take photographs or cut pictures out of magazines of activities you want to attempt to do. You can then put the photo of you doing it next to it once you have achieved that goal. Now that I'm a year and a half down the line I feel that this would have been of huge value to me. It is so easy at this stage to beat yourself up about how little progress you feel you're making; it is only when someone reminds me of what I've actually achieved. Only the other day a friend said, 'Don't you remember how long it took to get you downstairs and how many people had to help you and how you had to be helped out of bed and nurses needed to dress you?' By having photographic reminders you will feel so good reflecting on all your personal achievements so far and the many more to come.

When you are doing your physio practice on your own it is also valuable to remember. By looking at film you can compare your movements week by week and see the improvements. Is your walking more controlled and fluid? Are your movements more symmetrical? Do you look like you have more coordination? Again, if you consider horse trainers, they will watch horses on the gallops, tape every race meeting and then go home to study them; this is how they win races. We are striving for recovery and we will get there. We will achieve the best our body is capable of providing we put in the maximum effort. I'm also sure you can improve your speech by using a video and dictaphone (or modern equivalent). For me, when I was doing speech exercises, I needed to focus on something blank so that I wasn't trying to take too much in. It will be useful to ask your speech therapist about what could help you in particular.

Even now during conversations and trying to get the right words out, I need to focus sometimes on something blank rather than the person I am talking to.

As will now become apparent I can only recount my experiences and lessons throughout this journey and every stroke, every hospital will be different. However the overall message and goal remains the same for us all.

Things to remember:

- make home videos
- are there rugs, things you may trip over when you try to walk at home
- record future goals to work towards
- create a storyboard to look at and inspire you when you're alone

Chapter Three

My Hospital Experience

'If you do not hope you will not find what is beyond your hopes.'
St. Clement of Alexandria

Looking back now I can see that I must have been in denial. We had a skiing holiday booked and I wouldn't let Nick and Henry cancel it. In my mind I was still going skiing. Who was I kidding, I couldn't walk. But I told every nurse I was skiing. When I returned to hospital after my second stroke more than one member of staff mentioned my determination to go on that holiday. I remained somewhat distracted from the reality of the situation as if in a daze and thinking that everyone would soon realise I was fine and I would be discharged. They were all being over-cautious. I hadn't had a stroke just a migraine; it was all a misunderstanding.

For days afterwards I thought I would be going home. I told my poor son, Henry, 'they just need to confirm whether it's a clot or a bleed, give me a few tablets and we'll be off skiing'.
Then we were actually told it was a clot and possibly a complicated migraine as well which had also temporarily stopped the blood flow to my brain. Well this reality hit with a bang. Everything was so real, unknown and immeasurable to me now but I still kept on about the skiing as this gave me an immediate target. I was suddenly lost in this mess. I couldn't let go so I

33

needed a new goal even if it was totally unrealistic. I didn't have time to be ill; the holiday was booked. As I write now, I realise there was no logic to my reasoning but it became a prop to keep me positive about my recovery.

Everything had just crumbled, me, my job, my mobility, my role in life. I was transferred to the Stroke ward but I was still in denial. This is all part of the process of dealing with such a life-changing experience. Take as long as you need to come out of this stage whilst your brain gathers the tools to work out the best way to deal with and resolve the difficulties. It is important to know that as time passes, little by little, you will be able to come to terms with what has happened and find the best way to improve your situation and minimise the effects. You will stop feeling helpless.

My whole world had changed. I had always been pushing against time, rushing from one thing to another. Be careful what you wish for. I once wished I could have some time not having to work, just be at home without deadlines. Now I had all the time in the world everything was being done for me, in my bed, waking me up, washing me, feeding me at set meal times, giving me medication and then back to sleep. I didn't have to think about anything and I didn't. I just slept and slept and slept.

All the nursing staff were so helpful trying to make our bay in the ward as cheerful as possible, not an easy task. Another patient known as 'Bundle' was asleep even longer than me and was hugging her doll like a baby. Only June was up for conversation. I stayed in hospital for about a month and it was, only when I was moved to Rehab that I began to remember more about it. I recalled thinking how horrid the new ward smelled and saying to my friend Jackie that I didn't fancy eating any of my lunch as it hadn't smelled like this in the last place. Jackie quickly corrected me saying that Rehab was a distinct improvement. In fact this revealed that my sense of smell was returning and I hadn't even realised I'd lost it.

At first I didn't like it in Rehab as it seemed so serious and big with lots of beds in each bay. If you put us all in a bag and shook it you wouldn't get one fully-functioning human being. My few possessions had to be registered and accounted for which hadn't happened before. I had to be tested for MRSA. It was all so strict I felt I had done something wrong. None of us could get out of bed unaided. Every mouthful of food was recorded in our files to make sure we were eating enough. Friends brought in flowers and we longed for them to stay as they would have added a little much needed cheer to the place, but flowers were not allowed. I decided to lighten the mood a little. One day a friend brought an arrangement which we managed to pass off as high quality artificial flowers. They wilted eventually but the pleasure they gave my fellow inmates was immense and it revived the rebel in me.

How I longed for some fresh air and to get out of the ward for a while. This wasn't possible without a written request/consent form but luckily one Sister did allow a couple of friends to take me down to the garden. Kay and Jan put me in a wheelchair and we sat outside during visiting time. I was exhausted afterwards but it was brilliant. This was the start of my escapes. I longed for Kay and Jan to visit together. Or Jacques, Eamonn and Gaz so that I could go out to play.

One day I was all excited at going out but there was only one old wheelchair left with wheels that all worked independently. The nurse thought she should put a stop to this little trip and my heart sank. Then, before I knew it, Eamonn had put me in the wheel chair saying, 'Oh she's used to riding racehorses. Look at this'. And he neighed and we laughed and galloped out of the ward before the nurse could speak. Then we went further afield to the coffee shop so as not to be found, and later met Nick and my parents and had a tea party. When Henry took me back to the ward later on I felt like a naughty child as it was 5PM and way past hospital mealtime. Fortunately it was the right ward staff and they laughed with me and I was allowed out again.

The next time Jacques kept me out late and rang the ward bell, he considered running off and just leaving me so he wouldn't be told off. I would sometimes be wheeled over to June's bed before my own so I could smuggle her in a cake. She was my first friend in hospital as we were both in Stroke Ward and in Rehab although not next to each other in rehab which was a pity. We both felt the cold and had somehow been given permission to have duvets from home, which made my bed a little more welcoming. There had been televisions in Stroke Ward except we were too ill to watch them but not in Rehab as it was old; there was a small portable in the relatives' room which few of us could get into. As Cheltenham festival was looming, Nick and Henry brought me a laptop and set it up on the bedside table between Kath and me. The staff had set my ophthalmology tests for the start of the festival meaning I wouldn't be able to see a thing for the rest of the day, not even the food on my plate, they were not wrong. I missed it all. I could finally see again later that evening and was allowed to be wheeled to the restaurant for my first food since breakfast.

Our days started early by being woken for breakfast and medication at 7o'clock. Then we washed, etc. and waited for tests or visits from a doctor until our mid-morning drink and biscuits. It's amazing how exciting such a simple thing can become. We each had a time slot for our daily visit to the gym written on a board by the bed, obviously not the gym as we used to know it but in your bedclothes wheeled to a room full of hoists and bars. My slot lasted maybe fifteen minutes and at the end of that I'd feel tired. What has life come to? I had different coloured giant pegs which I had to try and open and they were by my bed all the time.

Look around your bedside table and find a packet or bag: anything that will make you practise little exercises with your weak hand. If it is under your nose and something you want to eat you will be forced to practise. For me it was the giant pegs on my packets of biscuits and chocolates so I had to use the damn things each time I wanted anything. There was another long wait until lunchtime but I have to admit I did sleep again most days and I always wondered why we had to be woken so early. The next clock watching would be for the 2.30 visiting time.

Things to remember:

- get people to take you off the ward at visiting time
- ask relatives, friends to bring things in that remind you of normality
- plan things that you would like to enjoy in the future

Chapter Four

Discharge from Hospital

'The thing always happens that you believe in, and the belief in a thing makes it happen.'
Frank Lloyd Wright

At last it was discharge day and I could finally leave Rehab and I could go home to Nick and Henry. It was the day I had been longing for. I couldn't wait to tell Nick and see Henry's surprise at finding me at home when he came back from school. I contacted Nick but he didn't respond in the way I imagined he would; naturally, I thought he would be as elated as me. Instead, he seemed to be very matter of fact as if I had called to say that visiting time had changed or some similar snippet of information. He also didn't appear to rush to fetch me. What I had failed to realise was that whereas I was so excited, for Nick it was as if his safety blanket had been removed. There had been no preparation for him, no talking through with him to check that he was ready for me to be at home which is not at all as he expected it to happen. The last he knew was that it would be at least a few more days, after all that is what we had been told. Then all of a sudden a call came that I was free to go. Up until then his days were broken up with drives to and from the hospital where he knew I was safe and cared for. Now it was different. I was Nick's responsibility and if there were any problems or complications it was up to him to act – all a little daunting when it was so unexpected. People also started to arrive at the house to fit equipment to make it easier for me to manage and inform Nick when staff would be visiting. It was a sudden overload and rather frightening. It was no wonder he didn't sound thrilled. I will just point out that when I did arrive home Nick had made it a superb homecoming with a banner and flowers.

I hope that before you leave hospital the occupational therapist will have either visited your home or discussed the layout of rooms with family members. Some people who lived just a couple of miles from the hospital were taken home with the occupational therapist before they were discharged where they could practise making a drink, move from room to room and identify what adaptations would need to be fitted before returning home. Following this they should organise other aids such as a seat and frame around toilets, bath rails and board where necessary or enlarging the shower. It depends on the area you live in and you may have an Intermediate Care Team working with you for a few months. If you are fortunate enough, they will also be able to add other devices to help you around your home. Admittedly, they don't look very pretty around the house but it makes the difference between managing and not managing. One thing that has proved priceless has been my trolley; it's quite an ugly contraption which you would usually associate with old people's homes, no disrespect intended, but I had not expected to rely on one in my forties. It is brilliant. I can make a drink and take it where I want and sit and drink it. This sounds simple but for those of you who are in my position know only too well that it's okay once you've mastered the art of making a drink but then it's either the stick or the drink, you can't take both! You can also use a thing called a grabber to help pick things up in the early days which is such a help in putting on socks, and all these things help you to regain your independence. A few months after first leaving hospital I was fitted with a device known as a leg lifter to help me with my drop foot. Although this had a slight benefit it wasn't really helping me. One thing I will say here is that we must all make sure we do not become too dependent on these and use them when we should be trying a little without them.

As you become more mobile you realise other obstacles are in your way. We have steps into our sitting room so when I could manage to get out of the chair and move I could not go into that room and lie down to sleep. Equally, if someone had put me in there for a sleep I couldn't get out until someone came back for me. Once I was able to be left alone for a couple of hours, I spent many months just sleeping in an arm chair in the kitchen because the floor between there and the cloakroom was flat. Our bedroom is exactly the same so I couldn't get out of the room once I had been put to bed. None of these dilemmas had been identified before I left hospital. I hated having to be dressed by someone else and having my clothes chosen for me. A huge part of my work before had been about image and fashion, having things look just right; now I was dressed as though I didn't care how I looked. Why is it

that every time the drawer was opened the closest pair of socks to the nurse's hand would be the furthest colour away from matching the colour of the top they had selected for me and the trousers too.

40

One day I was sitting in my chair and caught sight of the day's attire: green cords, purple socks and pink jumper with a different colour showing through the V of my jumper. I just hoped that no-one would come visiting me as I didn't want to give the impression that I had completely given up caring. All I needed to complete this new look was part of my lunch down my front; I felt and looked bad enough already. I fully understand how busy everyone is but if the colours did just blend a bit rather than scream out it would make us feel a bit better, don't you think? If it was done deliberately to force me to try harder to wash and dress myself then well done, it worked for me.

It is all about getting the right balance with safety and improvement. Sometimes this is when we need someone else to remind us that we should be doing things a little differently.

Others will help you find ways around hurdles. In time, the nurses found that I could get out of one door in the kitchen on sunny or dry days with my leg-lifter and walk around to the sitting room door if it was already unlocked and open so I could then sleep on the sofa rather than stay in the chair in the kitchen. I had to wear a bag with the phone in case I fell. Small things like that identified by your nurses or therapists and then practised eventually allow you more freedom and also help your confidence.

I am using a Functional Electronic Stimulator (FES) which I was given a few months after my second stroke. This improves walking for stroke survivors who have drop foot or other balance abnormalities gait. It is also used for people with multiple sclerosis, cerebral palsy, Parkinson disease and other nerve damage to

the spine or brain following head injury. I use the FES all the time along with my walking stick, when inside the house I am trying not to use my stick except when on uneven surfaces. My first reaction is to use it as it seems safer. When I am on an uneven surface it gives me greater stability and when I am around people walking at speed or without care as in a town then again it is helpful.

Following several attempts using equipment designed to help me walk, I was given the opportunity to try a basic version of the FES, which after it was determined successful I was referred to Selly Oak Rehabilitation Centre for a full assessment and fitting.

Functional Electrical Stimulation (FES) applies small electrical pulses to paralysed muscles to restore or improve their function through wires into electrodes put on the surface of the skin overlaying the muscles involved in a functional task. The electricity contracts the muscles in a precise pattern that allows for a specific task to be accomplished.

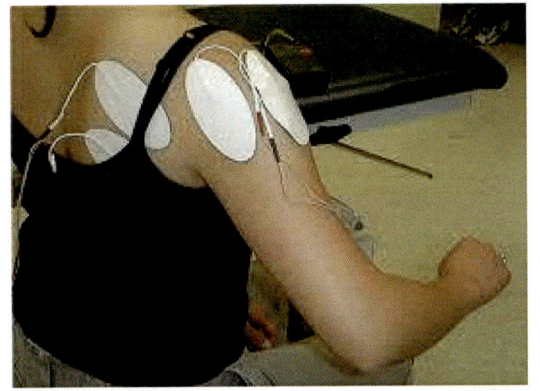

The basic model was a great success enabling me to attend the rehabilitation centre at Selly Oak, where I was fitted for a machine for use on my shoulder, arm and fingers and one for my leg and foot.

These appointments are detailed & lengthy because everyone's needs are so individual. Each time I have attended, the positioning of the electrodes has been adjusted slightly. A new photograph was taken to show me where to place them each day to keep the most beneficial

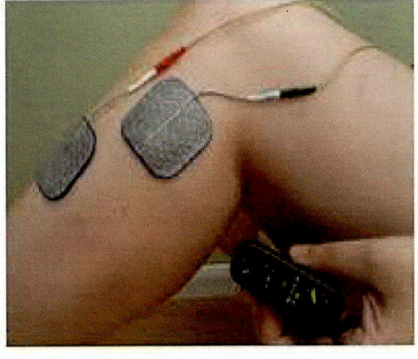

movement for me. Often the frequency of the machine has also been changed. These appointments are complex and make an incredible difference to quality of life, ease and mobility.

You can have varying types of machine and some are now even wireless but these are not available on the National Health. It is also possible to have an operation inserting part of the device into the muscle. I would have liked this for vanity reasons, although you still have to have the foot switch, which is the part attached to an insole and a box to control on & off plus frequency. Therefore it still is not completely invisible.

For women it is particularly difficult in the summer when it's hot and you would like to wear a skirt or shorts. I used to feel far too self-conscious to brave this especially as on trying I have been met with some very upsetting stares. These used to really upset me. Now I hold my head high and think they are the one with the problem, not me. I have been asked if I'm tagged, just escaped? I can now shake it off and laugh but don't get me wrong it has taken some time to get to this stage. I have also become very good at hiding as much of the device as possible.

A few tips for women:

- Take it out of its case and hide it in your bra, I have caused some laughs with this one on occasions with my sick humour. 'Oh I have to press my boob to get my leg to work'.

- In winter you can wear thick tights put the insole inside the tights; then wear long boots all wires are hidden and you can wear a dress.

- You can do the same as above with a skirt and clip the FES onto your waistband then hide with a top.

- You can have a different foot switch and short wires and get someone to remove clip from the back of the FES and replace with Velcro strap; you can then wear loose trousers such as linen and hide completely.

- You can remove the foot switch from the inner sole and tape it to a flat summer shoe so that you can wear something more normal and feel better.

- Hide the wires as normal under your trousers, then, rather than clipping the FES to your waist band, remove FES from its cover and hide in your pocket.

Things to remember:

- make sure family members ask all the questions they need to in preparation for your home coming
- make sure the family have support in place before your discharge as they will have concerns
- make sure your home is fully equipped for your return
- be aware how exhausting it is just to allow someone to get you up, wash you and feed you
- get lots of sleep; it is very important

Chapter Five

Bringing a Little Normality Back into Your Life

'When one door of happiness closes, another opens, but so often we look so long at the closed door, that we do not see the one that has been opened for us.'
Helen Keller

As you slowly get back to your usual routine, albeit little by little, think things through. I was so intent on getting back to normal that I didn't consider the effect it was having on my partner, Nick. Well, that's not totally true. I believed I had thought it through and that he would be pleased, but I had suddenly changed the dynamics of everything without warning. We had been getting along in this new forced routine with Nick doing all the shopping and cooking. Then, without discussing anything I planned a week's meals. I did this with the help of Headway, a tremendously supportive organisation, which took me shopping and helped me plan. I cooked supper for the next two evenings. I felt this was all positive stuff and a huge change for the better, but I had suddenly taken something from Nick that he was doing very well. He had been looking after us all for months in what was somewhat unknown territory for him and he had been in total control; I had taken all that away overnight. We, the stroke survivors, have ongoing discussions with therapists and support staff; our families don't have this opportunity so they are comparatively isolated. They shy away from discussing things with us as they feel we have enough to cope with already. But it is so important to sit down and discuss what your joint goals are. What would make your partner happy?

If you work at writing your goals together, you are not suddenly taking something away from your partner that they enjoy doing for you. It is far more frightening for them as they feel more out of control than we do. So the daily chore of preparing a meal became a comfort, something Nick had control over from start to finish.

Believing I was starting to look better helped me personally but equally had the adverse effect as Nick appeared to be less attentive. One day we arrived somewhere; he got out of the car and left me! He explained that it was more difficult now as I looked more like my old self and he expected the old me; he wanted me to be able to get out of the car and walk over to watch our son play cricket. Then, as the evening went on and I became tired and my speech slurred it was another reminder that the 'old me' wasn't totally back yet. It is easy to become so focused on your own improvement that you lose sight of what it's doing to those close to you.

Sleep and its Importance

It almost goes without saying that our bodies need sleep for our well-being but never more than now. We already know that the body repairs best when sleeping. Stroke survivors need far more sleep than most. It is believed that as we create a new brain circuit to compensate for the part of our brain killed off by the stroke, we use more energy which tires us. This is why it is not at all uncommon for stroke survivors to keep falling asleep, especially in the days immediately after the stroke. This tiredness now becomes a way of life.

47

As someone who was always on the go, full of energy and never fatigued, I found this particularly hard to come to terms with. How, at my age, could I become tired after just having a wash and eating my breakfast? If I were to stop being so hard on myself and simply analyse everything it would all be logical – I am recovering and at the moment I have to strive harder to achieve simple mobility.

As I'm progressing and improving I've found a way around things. It is simply accepting and planning. If I wish to have a meal with friends then I have a choice. I either stay in bed all morning or go back to bed in the afternoon; this way I'm able to do something normal in the evening. As far as writing this book is concerned, it is my wish to do so and I have every intention of completing it. But, I've realised I can't put a time scale on it as I may get up one day wanting to write only to fall asleep on the computer.

Fatigue

Severe fatigue affects a high percentage of stroke survivors, including me. It is hurtful at times, such as when a friend misunderstood and asked if I was depressed. They think, 'It's now nearly two years, so you shouldn't be feeling tired any longer'. But, sadly, if it's how the stroke has left you it is hard to fight. Try to console yourself with knowing how much you've improved. There are many different reasons for extreme fatigue:

- all the nurses working with you and the ongoing therapy
- you're using much more energy now even to do very simple tasks
- your muscles are weaker
- it's more difficult for you to communicate

- you're often in pain
- you have difficulty sleeping
- you're on medication
- you may be worrying, especially if you're living alone
- you may be depressed
- an area of your brain may be damaged
- you may be dehydrated

Some of these symptoms improve with time. Dehydration is easily resolved, but only if someone else steps in. A stroke survivor may well forget to frequently take a drink of water, so this is difficult if a lot of time is spent alone. This may sound ridiculous to someone who has not suffered brain injury but, even now as I'm writing this book, if my tablets are not put up for me in the morning I will not remember to take them. Logic is not what it was. This is why it can be stressful for someone living on their own, a real risk of them missing their medication. To help, you can ask your GP for a blister pack which organises your daily medication throughout each week.

Back to beating fatigue – one way, believe it or not, is exercise. If you can build up some muscle strength again and rest sufficiently after exercise; and also eat well, you will thus create a healthy balance.

Bath Time

During recovery we're told to shower rather than bathe, as it's easier and something we may be able to manage on our own. But not for me; I've never been a shower person. I have always enjoyed a bubbly bath with a book in one hand and a glass of wine at my side. So, for me, this was another step back to normality, that is, once I was in. I have not yet reached the stage of the book or the drink but, just to be immersed in bubbly water is such a wonderful feeling. It was fantastic the first time and still is. Hot bubbly water and a scented candle with soothing music are all feel good factors. You can also use a loofah or sponge to massage your affected arm or leg. Always massage upwards towards the heart and finish on a part of your body not affected by the stroke, for example, from your fingertips to your shoulder. This is valuable as well as being enjoyable, because it transmits a positive message to the brain reminding it that these limbs are still connected. If you are a shower person, then you can adapt it to suit, but make sure you follow your physiotherapist's guidelines to ensure you don't fall.

There are several options here. You can opt for a bath board but that only allows you to put your feet in the bath. (It is great for resting your drink on, though.) Or you can have an electric chair that lowers you down. In my case, I'm fortunate to be female, smaller than my partner so he can lower me in and out. Whoops! Now the Intermediate Care Team (ICT) knows I lied, although I think they guessed already.

Personality Changes

This one is a bit of an eye-opener and a little unnerving at times. Right now, I don't know if this is temporary or long-term. For instance, I can watch a familiar film which hasn't particularly moved me and now I'm in tears. I can also have a conversation with someone and various, tactless thoughts run through my head which I would normally keep to myself or find a careful way of expressing them. But, now, there doesn't seem to be an analytical, protective bit in my brain to filter my words and they just spill out. My friend,

Eamonn, jokes about it as my post-stroke personality, but at the same time says, 'About bloody time!' Maybe now I will stop allowing those people I'm talking about walking all over me. True to form, they are not around now.

Personalities are often changed post-stroke – you may be more emotional, emotionless or depressed. No two strokes are exactly the same, but we do tend to fall into one of these categories. Over half of stroke survivors will feel depressed at times, and if this is severe, you will need the support of a good GP. One member of my Brain Group suffered in silence for too long and found everything much easier once he'd asked for help. The sudden life changes and day-to-day difficulties after a stroke will be depressing but, on top of these, are the different ways our brains have been affected; it is not a fault or weakness. If the stroke was on the right side of the brain it can mean the person may be less able to show emotion than used to be the case, and this might be misinterpreted as depression. These are some of the signs to look out for, some of which are predictable and temporary; others will warrant talking to your nurse or GP:

- feeling continually low, having no motivation, sad
- feeling worthless, having no self-esteem
- worrying a lot, anxious
- finding it difficult to sleep
- not being interested in anything
- unable to concentrate
- having no interest in food

Your doctor will be able to identify whether it is best to help you with medication or counselling. Sometimes all that is needed is a bit more normality with friends, family and everyday activities. You may need both but, either way; the situation can be resolved easily.

Emotional Liability

This can be even more difficult for the family members than the stroke survivor. It is when the survivor shows sudden changes of emotion that they are not aware of. They might start laughing or crying for what appears to be no reason, or suddenly become very angry. They may be very angry one minute, then suddenly start laughing for no apparent reason. This condition can put a lot of stress on families and relationships.

One example of this, that I experienced was during my stay in Rehab where there was a man who we felt sorry for, but at the same time we were unnerved by his belligerent and unpredictable behaviour, as he was stronger than most of the staff. His wife also found this very difficult to cope with, especially since he was unaware of the distress he was causing to others. He would suddenly become angry and aggressive towards us all which when your mobility is restricted is very frightening. We later learnt, sadly, his behaviour was too difficult for his wife to deal with and, like many couples affected by brain injury, it ended in divorce.

Things to remember:

- develop a daily routine and prepare for sleep at night
- celebrate all/any achievements
- resolve to adapt to this new lifestyle
- time and/or antidepressants can help

Chapter Six

Rehabilitation at Home

'Nothing at all can stop the man with the right mental attitude; nothing at all can help the man with the wrong mental attitude.'
Thomas Jefferson

Following a stroke, most survivors are hospitalised, then assigned a care package for when they go home. However, it does depend on where you live. In my area there is an Intermediate Care Team and they came out to my home from the very first day for twelve weeks and every day. Normally the Promoting Independence Team would have taken over after six weeks but, due to complications, they didn't, so the
Intermediate Care Team stayed to avoid my being stranded. They were made up of nurses, physiotherapists and occupational therapists, and all were amazing; I could not have wanted for better care and support.

The icing on the cake was when Jane came in as one of the team – she was an old friend of mine from junior school days. She was with me every week, worked me hard, motivated me and didn't let me slack. Quite by chance, on one Friday afternoon she had changed her shift time and that was the day of my second stroke. It was happening as she arrived and she had the ambulance there quickly and travelled with me on the way to the hospital. She tells me we travelled so fast that, even strapped in, she felt too young to go flying! I had ICT twice a day for the following weeks and even on weekends and holidays. It is a tremendous emotional and remedial support.

Power of the Mind – Determination

This is probably our most powerful recovery tool, for without this we are lost and our progress limited, if not halted. Recovering from a stroke is a huge test of our personal strength and commitment to ourselves. In my case, I had always put others' needs before my own so it was a new experience in many ways. But, if we are not careful, we can run the risk of becoming selfish. We need to maintain the determination to get better and work on ourselves every day, but also be aware of our limitations and not push ourselves too far. Otherwise we could become unwell and then stop any progress for a while. Stroke is definitely a test in every sense of the word but I believe it is a condition that allows the individual a high percentage of control over their own recovery, and that is a good ailment to be burdened with.

People will help and advise you who are very knowledgeable in their field. They may, however, say some things that are difficult to hear or that you disagree with. For instance, I was told that a person who has a heart attack either dies or survives and if survives, lives life as normal. But, with a stroke, a person either dies or survives and lives life with a disability and life is never the same. Those comments almost made me lose my focus. My brother, Tom, suggested that the lady was talking from numerous years of experience and was trying to prepare me by illustrating that people can return to work, even with disabilities. He reminded me that she cannot talk from personal experience of having a stroke or understand where I am coming from with my belief. But he said, 'Do not judge her for this, let it go, hold on to what you believe'. However, I remember this distinctly and as it was not said from a stroke survivor's experience, it did take me some time to act on my brother's advice. I, on the other hand, won't let go of my belief and I'm not prepared to settle for second best. I have not given up the idea of going skiing; it won't be this year and it probably won't be next, but it will be one year. I am determined to return to my former self. It is hard work but my personality is such that I cannot and will not give up.

The sheer fact of having a stroke means so much about you, and your life has changed. You have lost your identity and need to reclaim as much as possible. Self-confidence and image are so important to you. Someone who was a businessman, a manager, in fashion or in a fulfilling job is suddenly being dressed by nurses and is possibly unable to speak. Everything that made you feel confident has been stripped away. It can leave you feeling vulnerable, inadequate, frustrated or angry. This is why it is so important to help the stroke survivor with their appearance.

Some simple examples that a carer can do that will make a difference are:

- wash and blow-dry the person's hair
- give the person a shave (if male)
- do up their shirt buttons correctly
- put on the shoes they like to wear
- get them an enjoyable book or magazine to read when they can
- put on their makeup and paint their fingernails
- put on their favourite jewellery, necklace and earrings

- take them with you to collect the children from school

These are just a few things that allow the person to be who they were before and that give them more confidence in going out in public.

It is also important to remember that just because they are recovering you must not shut them out of family decisions. Unbeknown to the family members, this is done in all families because they believe they're trying to protect their loved one. Families are very busy, but try to involve the stroke survivor in decisions. Find tasks for them that are achievable but which still make them feel needed. Remember to continue to ask the survivors advice as you would always have done to help them feel included, not overloaded.

Things to Consider to Aid Recovery

After the world you find yourself thrown into, the last thing you'd think you'll want is photographs of yourself; but now that it is too late for me we have realised the value of a video diary. This has been substantiated by an email friend of mine, Paul, a fellow stroke sufferer in NZ. His physiotherapist did exactly that. I am repeating what he said because it is so important: 'I ask you to think hard - is there really a reason not to do this? The help it will give you along your journey outweighs those reasons you have just aired. Remember I would've used those very same ones, but I see how the benefits are stronger. On those days you don't feel you are making much progress - all that effort for little reward - then someone pops the video on for you and you can see the progress you have made in that past week, two weeks, whatever it might be. I found I am so focused on my next goals all the time I've forgotten what I have achieved. It is only when a nurse comes in, who hasn't been here for a week or more and they say, 'Wow, look at that your foot, it isn't so turned in' or 'You are moving another finger', it can be anything but for someone to notice and pass comment, that is wonderful'.

Within your video record make reference to all your firsts. For example, when you first hold a tooth brush; made your lunch, a sandwich, unaided; a drink; got out of the chair alone, etc. They are all huge milestones in our new strange world we find ourselves launched into.

The next few pages are your Personal Record and future help so please use them in a journal or notebook. Initially you might look and think it is the last thing you wish to do, but I speak from experience when I say I wish I had thought of it and done so.

You may need to ask for assistance to complete the following pages, which I have deliberately left blank for you and I suggest you return to them often. I promise, as you look back over the months and read through the entries, you will not be able to help but realise how much you have improved. So make that first entry now, however small it may feel. For example, you managed to clean your teeth or make a drink.

Personal Record

Medication:

Name of tablet - Dosage - Time taken

My personal risk factors are:

For example, this could be high cholesterol, high blood pressure. List also what you can personally change to reduce the risk of future problems.

1)

2)

3)

4)

5)

Notes your occupational therapist or friend helping you may wish to add:

Photographs:

Now this needs to be a double page because here it is important to have both photographs of how you are now and also photographs of things you want to be able to do. On the second list it may be to hold a cup or stand unaided, but put them in because when you achieve them the feeling is second to none.

Goals:

Here it is both important to list your goals and also to leave space for a date for the simple reason that at such time you are able to achieve that goal you can record it.

Timeframe:

Date of entry - Date achieved

Questions and Answers:

You may ask why this one is in here when it is for your record. If you do not need it then just skip over it, but all along I have had difficulty with remembering what I needed to ask the specialist when I saw her next. Also what the answer was to any question I had asked. I was concentrating so much on trying to ask my next question I had not absorbed the answer to the former one. So for me something like this would have been very helpful. As when questions arise someone could have completed this for me and also written down the answers following visits to the specialist or doctor.

Question:

Answer:

Question:

Answer:

Question:

Answer:

You may want to ask someone to photocopy these pages to take with you to your next appointment.

Feelings and Emotions

Now this is a tough one and you may choose to skip over it, but it could be a good way to help each other through this tough situation we are all thrown into. You could just say that whatever you enter is in everyone's best interest!

Words You Keep Hearing: Quality not Quantity...Let me do that for you

I have been so determined all the way through, each time achieving one goal, immediately creating a new one. This is something that is valuable but unlike me, stop and reward yourself for each achievement. All our goals will be individual and thus different.

Mine was to be able to wash and dress myself unaided, having finally achieved this I was now, capable of being left alone for a while between treatments.

Rather than be satisfied with this achievement I pushed myself for my next one which was to make a hot drink and lunch. We had practised making hot drinks in hospital in preparation for returning home and I had my disabled trolley provided by the Intermediate Care Team (ICT) so I didn't have to carry the cup anywhere. I believed this small task to be something I was capable of, I was wrong, I ended up scalding myself, needing daily treatment for a nasty scald.

This is a prime example of why we need to pace ourselves and not push too hard, but once the hand had healed I still needed to prove to myself that I could make something to eat. It was to be a banana sandwich which I had worked out I could break and squash inside sliced bread, which pre stroke would have sounded quite disgusting, but I was elated, I had made it unassisted and it tasted amazing and ended up being lunch for many days to follow.

The ICT Team brought loads more gadgets into my home which meant I could open my tablet bottles, the helping hand device to help put socks on; a foot lifter to help me get over steps; a grab for picking things up off the floor and several aids to help in the kitchen. They identified which things would make everyday tasks possible. I have found a can opener that I can operate with just one finger, so I can now move on to tuna sandwiches.

I found it very difficult to accept all these aids which I felt reinforced my disability. One of my biggest hurdles was accepting a disabled badge. I held off and held off until I had sense talked into me and eventually ran out of excuses. It sounds silly as I put it on paper but I did not want to be called disabled for fear of it becoming permanent. Permanent just isn't in my plan and goal mind set, so it frightened me. It damaged my strong belief in getting better. Anyway, I finally got over that one too and now quite happily slap it on the windscreen, relieved to be able to park somewhere close, which means I too can go inside like everyone else.

During your recovery it is important not to fall into the mind set, 'Now I am disabled', as some organisations choose to use this phrase.
Personally I feel it hinders recovery. Instead of focusing on your disability, focus on your abilities. What you can do today that you couldn't do last week. People often forget or don't even realise that stroke survivors can still think, feel and hear. They are as intellectually aware as they were pre-stroke and

this is where a great deal of the frustration comes from. Especially if a person cannot vocalise their thoughts at the moment.

Going out for the First Time

This can be exhausting both mentally and physically. If the person doesn't feel quite ready, then don't force it. It may be advisable to make the first visit to a friend's house so they are in familiar and comfortable surroundings. This could include interacting with someone they haven't met before to be slightly out of their comfort zone.

I found it very difficult when I first went into a shop. A lot of time had passed and I thought I was prepared for anything, but when asked, 'Oh, you poor thing, what happened to you?' I was at a loss for words. I couldn't move an inch and then I just couldn't bring myself to say I'd had a stroke; I suddenly felt like a freak on show. I eventually said it and felt my eyes welling up, so I made my way back to the car which, thanks to having a disabled badge, was just outside. I had previously been shopping in a wheelchair and this was so difficult. I was at the wrong height and I couldn't see anything and so felt more noticeable. Yet, at the same time you feel as if you're invisible as some people choose not to help you. They are all new experiences you have to adjust to.

Now, nearly two years on, I am much stronger and it rarely bothers me if someone asks. I simply say, 'Oh, I had a stroke.' If they say, 'Oh, you're too young', I reply, 'No, people much younger than me have had strokes' or, 'There is always someone who's worse off than me.'

Sometimes, however, it is frustrating as there is a certain type of person, sadly women, in my own experience, who choose to ignore me if I am looking in their shops. Previously, they would have greeted me with the usual, 'Oh, can I help you?' Now, I just frequent different shops, in the words of *Pretty Woman*, 'Big mistake'. They are the ones with the problem, not us.

Sometimes, too, people's reactions can make you laugh. My friend and occupational therapist Jane, realised I'd been cooped up in my kitchen for months, and decided to take me to a local garden centre for my rehab session to let me try walking on a different surface. We were greeted by the girl who worked there with a friendly welcome followed by, 'Oh no, what have you fallen off now?' The previous year I had parted company with (fallen off) a racehorse and ended up rather broken. Jane pointed out that in a funny sort of a way it was a compliment; and it was a turning point for me as I was then able to talk about it without being upset.

Going out also puts pressure on the carer as they are aware of how uptight and nervous you may be feeling but, equally, they have the responsibility for your well-being: Finding out where to park, how quickly you tire, wondering how long you should stay out, what to do if you become upset and don't want to get out of the car. Do they have to push you, or just return home? They have to put themselves in your shoes yet at the same time show confidence, encouragement and strength. They haven't been given a manual (until now) on how best to handle things if we bottle it or become tired or unwell. I often think it is worse for the carers since they cannot know how we are feeling or how much we are hiding; they have to guess and have all that responsibility.

Going it alone – Confidence

Going out alone is still something I haven't fully managed, even three years after my stroke. Having the confidence to venture out on my own is a huge thing for me, I feel so vulnerable and it is still too daunting. I feel that if people walk past me very quickly and bump into me they can very easily knock me over. If I were on my own I wouldn't be able to get up and it would also be very easy for the wrong person to steal my purse, etc. It is sad to have to think this way but we have to be realistic in today's society. I am not able to drive and unable to get on a bus by myself, which is why I haven't ventured out on my own. We live in a remote area so I'm not in a situation where I can just walk into a coffee shop or public space.

It is strange to recollect that during the pre-stroke days I'd think nothing of jumping into a car, driving wherever I needed, entering any room and not be phased by any situation or group of people. I remember a lady once saying to me that she was too nervous to drive on a motorway and would drive many extra miles to avoid doing so. I didn't let my surprise show for fear of hurting her feelings, but I could not comprehend her logic, how she would drive all those miles and waste all that time when all she was afraid of was another road. Yet I now understand how something so seemingly simple and straightforward for most of us can be a real difficulty for some.

Simple things such as going to social events take a great deal out of me; apart from the fatigue there is all the planning to be able to cope. When you go somewhere you are offered a drink and there are people to mingle with. This is your first obstacle: Do you decide to drink and stay in that one place, so you don't accidentally spill it, until the occasion is all over? This is all well and good as long as the other person doesn't decide to mingle and leave you all alone. Your second choice is to mingle yet stand out as not joining in because you don't have a drink and everyone keeps reminding you, so you have to explain why, time and time again.

I know these are little things but they all add to the stress of a situation and for some people become the reason for not going out at all. I'd advise you to fight this and go out as often as you can; it will get easier and it also becomes easier to explain the difficulties with less discomfort. Do try it sooner rather than later as the longer you avoid it the more difficult it will become. It doesn't bother me now that when I go out with friends, however basic or smart the place, someone takes my plate from me and cuts up my food, as they would with a child, and hand it back to me; I almost don't notice any longer. I can still join in and have a good time and feel much better on returning home than I did before going out, even on those days when I didn't feel like doing anything.

Things to remember:

- celebrate every achievement irrespective of how small
- don't rush onto your next goal too soon, it's quality not quantity of achievement
- make video records of your achievements

Keep a personal record of:

- your medication: name of tablet - dosage - time taken

- your personal risk factors

- notes by your occupational therapist or friend

- photographs

- goals

- feelings and emotions

- questions for your doctor and/or therapist

- don't be afraid to venture out of your home, it's exhausting but rewarding

Chapter Seven

The Effect on Me

'A stumbling block to the pessimist is a stepping stone to the optimist.'
Eleanor Roosevelt

Think of a stroke as giving you an advantage over others. Yes, I did say 'advantage'. When else would you be given the luxury of time to reflect on your working life and life in general and re-evaluate and ask what really matters and what doesn't?

Henry, my son, illustrated this by saying although the stroke has caused some tough and lonely times it has made us stronger as individuals and as a family unit. So possibly you could say 'stroke struck but together we're stuck'.

I recently managed to go to the last part of my son's Sports Day and am proud to say I was sitting by the finishing line as he won his race. Friends came over to me and were lovely. In days of old pre-stroke days, I would have missed that event and that proud moment. One mother came over with a friend of mine and it was the first time I had seen her since my stroke. She talked solidly about herself for at least five minutes, then made her exit. My friend and I both felt we needed to take a breath for her, and had such a giggle afterwards as she seemed oblivious to all that was happening around her. This later made me realise that some people, however well you know them, may feel uneasy, not know what questions to ask, or feel nervous so, if they cannot avoid you, talk "ten to the dozen" about the first thing that comes into their head. Sadly, until you process it, there are some people out there who are a little heartless.

Perhaps some people need to forget designer labels, flashing cash, and talking about their next social event - then have a reality check and visit rehab and experience, just for a couple of hours, what it's like for us to try and hold a cup of coffee or answer a phone. I don't mean to sound bitter. I just want people to wake up and realise what really matters and appreciate what they have rather than be miserable about what they don't have.

Okay, yes, we've got a huge uphill struggle, but how else in our lives would we have a chance like this? Yes, I did say chance. Life is often so busy that we find ourselves working too hard in jobs we don't enjoy, or in other areas of our life where we know we should slow down. We just don't admit it or can't justify changing. This is an opportunity to look at life afresh, to ask ourselves openly and honestly what we'd really like to do, perhaps even retrain. All the previous pressure we had every day has been removed. This can be exciting.

Another time I was with my son and his girlfriend and they were watching a TV reality show. Well, my head was like the sky on bonfire night. People were airing their problems so openly about why your man cheats on you and how to get him to spend more time on you by losing weight, improving your appearance. Whether male or female, as you read this you will know that a stroke does all the above. You lose weight and for us girls it's fabulous for our nails, and our partner spends so much time on us, although not quite how they intended on the television. When something as catastrophic as a stroke happens it affects your whole view of life and also that of your family. It is a poignant message about what really matters.

My sympathy level has totally changed – if you don't like something, don't moan, do something about it. Look at the positive. Recently, someone was complaining about feeling tired as she'd walked the dog early and done a day's work, that day being 10 till 4, which in my book was only half a day. However, she was moaning to me, the one who longed to be able to get out of my chair and perform the simple task of walking, aided or otherwise, from one end of my kitchen to the other. I'm tired and can't do any of those things. I pointed out to her how lucky she was. 'You can walk, drive and work what do you really have to complain about?' She just didn't get it and continued finding fault. At that point I gave up and realised there was no point in thinking I could have a meaningful conversation with her.

This person, whom I once considered a friend, is no longer in my life, which was her choice, not mine. She began to take advantage of my situation and the new, unwell me, and changed. This is something we need to be aware of and rather than allowing it to end in an argument, as I did, in retrospect I should have just removed myself from the situation. You need support and encouragement, not negativity and upset; you deserve more. As a friend pointed out to me, on more than one occasion, you only need your real friends around you at the moment.

I have had hours of thinking time which has been a huge learning curve. Looking back at myself in the pre-stroke days I have realised that I do not want to return to being that person, so bothered about being late, driving too fast to reach somewhere on time, worried about the house being a mess if visitors came and noticed the clothes drying on the radiators. Now, I ask myself, 'What was all that about?' With our home occupied by nurses, occupational therapists, physios and friends helping me to wash and dress, all that is long forgotten. Priorities change and I would like to think I have become a more relaxed and better person.

Along with letting go of the things that don't matter you realise the value of true friends. Your family is there for you and is tremendously special, but friends have a choice. There is no written rule that they have a role to play in this situation that confronts you. My true friends stayed, and they have been with me the whole journey. I will admit that I feel emotional while writing this; I could write a book on the love and support shown to me by them from the very beginning, wheeling me off to
escape from the ward for a while, continuing support in home visits and phone calls when away, texts and emails when on holiday or working away, and getting cross or firm with me when I needed it. You all know who you are and I thank you for your kindness throughout. Being thrown into this situation just shows you how good humanity really is, and believe me it is. I have had lovely messages and acts of kindness from people I barely know, and have crossed a few off my Christmas list whom I thought I did know. Psychologically, it felt good to dump them, so, Eamonn, you were right. I reflected on a part of work where some people only have small parts, some are in the whole show, life is the same.

None of us would wish to be in this situation, but I have learned that I need to re-evaluate my work and what I expect of my body and myself. Hence, my stroke of luck.

Things to remember:

- focus on what you can benefit from
- do not dwell on 'Why stroke, why me'
- look for the positives you can take from the situation

Chapter Eight

Effect the Stroke had on My Family

'The more difficulties one has to encounter within and without the more significant and higher in inspiration his life will be.'
Horace Bushnell

At the beginning you and your family are at opposite ends of a bridge, all having different lessons to learn, all equal in difficulty, all understanding the need to ask for help and learning how to communicate with one another again, each confronted by different dilemmas and decisions. The family has just been dealt with a bombshell; their loved one has been taken from them and replaced with a stranger who only just resembles the person they once loved.

All of you need help to make sure each other's needs and feelings are understood. All of you have been thrown into this new and confusing situation headfirst, in many ways it is worse for the carer. They have to just look on and watch what has happened to someone they love as well as look after them once they are home, and do all the things you both used to do, and somehow keep smiling!

There are leaflets out there such as *A Carer's Guide* explaining that when someone close to you has had a stroke they may need extra support, etc. I am not knocking that but I am yet to find the leaflet truly covering the needs and questions required by the carer. What about their support? They have also been thrown into this horrid new situation headfirst and suddenly have new responsibilities, alongside normal everyday duties, and they have had a bereavement. They have, as already mentioned, lost the person they have always known and loved. They have a great deal to come to terms with. How do you explain to carers that puzzling behaviour isn't simply a reaction to stroke, it is a devastating calamity, a direct result of brain damage. There is a rising number of stroke survivors in their forties according to recent findings, and women migraine sufferers are three times more likely to suffer a stroke especially those approaching menopause.

Crying is also part of the recovery process; don't fight it, greet it. I fought it, I felt I had lost control of enough already I didn't want to add to this list by now losing control of my emotions and becoming tearful. I had a natural tendency to fight it. Learn from my mistake: It is important to accept this emotion, greet it, allow it in and embrace it fully, and allow the tears to flow. This is an important part of the healing process. We are after all experiencing bereavement. It is the loss of our former self and life. This however must be explained in full to the carer's family members so that they understand and don't suddenly begin to question their actions or care they are giving the survivor.

Depending on your age and stage in life you are possibly now as I was in a situation where your work and income too have gone overnight. This in itself is another huge blow. I am self-employed, I do not have any insurance

74

policies in place, so yet another reminder of the independence lost. Driving is something I am no longer allowed or able to do, so again another loss of independence. Rather than allow myself to get down over this I have chosen to view it as an opportunity; time for me. I am making time for me. I will re-evaluate things; I will be back, this is just an interval. All sorts of fortuitous happenings and opportunities come to play and come to help you along the way. Don't dwell on what's happened, lost opportunities in the past, look at what will give you happiness, satisfaction in the future.

A friend explained to me; funnily enough just prior to my second stroke. Hold on to the thought of a new house theory; which is that I may have currently knocked the old one down but the foundation still remains; it is in place for me to build something stronger. So if I feel myself dwelling on things I think about Eamonn's new house theory. Also that age does not come into this - we are never too old to recover from a stroke, it is all down to our PMA (positive mental attitude).

Facing and Dealing with the Future for the Carer

For the carer this is new unknown territory. You are the one now being mum, dad, partner and carer. Where in all of that is there time for you? Make time for you. Allow help, don't let pride get in the way.

Remember, you have not been professionally trained for this new role, but have been thrown in at the deep end, so it is not at all unusual, or wrong, to experience feelings of anger, resentment, loss, inadequacy, fear, anxiety, and/or depression. You are, after all, carrying out the roles you both previously shared, along with being the carer and coping with the

75

bereavement of your previous life together. You are probably being strong for your children and also still holding down a job. Also, if you are male (sorry guys) you will be refusing the offers of help because of pride. If female, perhaps you suddenly have to handle all the finances that your husband previously did, not knowing where files or accounts are, or when bills need paying, which are all very daunting.

A stroke is a huge shock to all involved so you haven't had time to prepare for this, and what's ahead, so for that reason be kind to yourself. Do not expect to get it right every time; it isn't possible. You, your partner, your family will be finding new ways of dealing with things. It is natural for you to feel a sense of loss, grief, anger, resentment, anxiety or depression. You may experience all of these emotions and many others, it is normal. It does not mean you are a bad person or you are not coping; quite the opposite it probably means you are trying so hard you are over worrying, putting extra stress on your already stressful load. Your whole life after all has already been changed by the stroke.

The following tips are from both experienced counsellors and carers who have come out the other side:

- Talk to The Stroke Association and/or Headway; both have counselling services available for carers and siblings.

- Make sure you have time for you and your interests; i.e., go to the gym, play golf, go for a walk, read a good book, socialise with friends. When you do this, you are not abandoning your partner but allowing yourself time to recharge your batteries, relax and remember who you are outside your carer's role. By allowing yourself to do this you will be both happier and stronger, thus better able to help your partner on your return. So keep that in mind if guilt starts to creep in whilst you are out having fun. Remind yourself it is beneficial to you all as a family unit that you do this.

- Be honest to yourself and someone else about your feelings, a friend or a counsellor, preferably someone qualified or who knows you well. You won't feel strong all the time. You will have times when you feel you are sinking, everything is too much, 'Why me?' This isn't bad but normal; you are human, this situation is daunting.

- Accept help, people offer because they mean it, they want to help. If you keep saying no and pushing them away eventually those offers of help will stop. Sometimes people enjoy helping; think of it that way next time someone asks, 'Shall I do the ironing for you?' Or 'I am going shopping, what do you need?' Say 'Yes. Please'.

Recently, my partner Nick was juggling the usual: me to and from appointments, our son Henry to and from school and cricket matches and in between getting the shopping done and feeding us all. Is it no wonder he accidentally filled our diesel car up with regular petrol?! Mistakes like this, I believe, are quite a common occurrences for carers. You may well identify with this as you read on? It is a sign they need to slow down and look after themselves; have that time out doing what they enjoy. For us it is also the cruel reminder that you cannot relieve your partner of some of those pressures, but instead are the cause of a high percentage of them. It is a double edged sword; it makes both the carer and the stroke survivor feel bad about themselves when really we should both say we are both doing the best we can here, and we didn't need or choose this. Leave it at that rather than dwell on what we can't do or should have done; it is human nature, adding extra stress to an already stressful situation.

Start Off as You Mean to Go On

For the benefit of the carer, before the stroke survivor leaves the hospital, make sure you have a care plan in place and that it is one that you have confidence in. Make sure you are clear on how you and the patient are going to function at home. What devices will be in place and what help will be provided? Also, that you feel both clear and confident coping with what is ahead of you; and if you do not then simply ask for it to be explained more clearly. If adaptations are not fitted at home you cannot cope, so they need to be in place first. Staff on the wards deal with strokes daily; it is very easy for them to forget all that needs explaining; and they don't mind being asked. Caring for a disabled person at home is a very responsible and demanding role so take as much time as you need asking for help now. Be as prepared as you can, otherwise you are adding additional stress.

As a carer, draw up a rough list, in order, of daily tasks you have control over. This may appear a little strange, but as you begin your daily routine you will see its importance both for you and the survivor, as they will benefit by having a routine.

For example, list the daily tablets and times they are to be given; time of getting up, washing, dressing the survivor, times other carers, physiotherapists or other visitors are coming in. Include the times of washing and blow-drying hair, putting on makeup, shaving, if a man (or legs, if a woman), preparing the survivors breakfast, lunch, dinner etc.

Don't forget having to shop and also carrying out your own daily tasks, which will include washing, cooking and ironing, which also have to be taken into consideration. Your list may be long, but with the importance of giving medication at the right times, it will help having it all written down.

You may be in a situation where you are also juggling a job or caring for children, with this role too, or in some cases all of the above. You may also now have additional stress regarding finances, as the person you are caring for could be the main provider in the household, or may have been earning and you relied on their income too. Everyone's situation is individual, but certainly as a carer your role is demanding, exhausting and daunting.

There are a few important points as a carer you should remind yourself of regularly:
Recognise it is normal to feel angry with the situation or person sometimes. Accept and expect help from others. Take care of yourself; keep your own interests/hobbies and feel content with the help you are giving even if you are not being shown gratitude. Do not question or judge your efforts, you are doing your best.

You will manage initially, but it will be taking its toll on you, and if you become unwell obviously that will not help either of you. You will become over tired which then can lead to grumpiness, poor sleep, and even depression.

Friends and relatives all rally round in the early stages and offer help, but as time goes on, especially if you have declined help, along with the person beginning to look visibly better, their offers drop off, and they just return to their daily lives; and you will find yourself having to cope alone.

Recognising and Dealing with Emotions

Anger and resentment: At times you will experience both of these emotions. You will feel angry towards the survivor and resentment too. This is normal; you are doing all within your power to look after and care for your partner; they may not appear grateful. They may not even notice; they may simply want more. You may resent them taking all your time and energy, preventing you from doing as you would normally do; they have taken your life away as you have known it the past years. This is all normal and natural and part of the grieving process. You have a bereavement of the person you fell in love with; you are now presented with a different version of that person; one you have to get to know and understand all over again, as well as care for. Just let these feelings in; accept them for what they are, give them a little attention, do not fight them, do not feel bad for having them. After a while begin to focus on happy times you shared as a couple; as a family things that make you feel good. Expand on that emotion and gradually release the other thoughts. In time this will become easier and they will fade completely; especially as you create more happy ones.

These feelings are exactly the same too for the children. All their lives they have had this parent to look up to, turn to, ask advice and help from. The parent who promised they would always be there for them; then suddenly one day everything changed. In Henry's case he went off to school for what

80

he believed would be a normal day; quite a fun one actually as he had a rugby match, only to return to discover life would never be quite the same at home. The mother who he had previously been able to rely on was soon to have to rely on him. A mother he barely knew; she could no longer string a sentence together, she was in a hospital and one side of her body refused to work. When she did begin to mutter things he could just about understand she promised him they were still going skiing. Who was this person?! In her mind she truly believed they would go skiing; she was in denial; to Henry, this person who had brought him up to believe you should never lie was doing exactly that, and to him. As if this wasn't bad enough, she did it a second time. What Henry did not understand was that following the second stroke she actually cried realising what had happened? One night during visiting time, Henry had decided to test if any feeling had returned in my foot, so he'd been constantly tapping it while sitting with me. He asked the question, 'Can you feel anything?' To which I replied; convinced and believing wholeheartedly this was the case, 'Yes, some feeling is definitely coming back'. Henry's face dropped in front of me, he had the look on his face that a disappointed parent gives a child when they have done wrong. He simply said, 'Well, I've been tapping on it since I arrived. How come you didn't say stop?' My heart sank, Henry thought I had lied. But my brain had tricked me again, until that moment I really believed some feeling had returned.

Although this experience will never leave me, it still saddens me even now, on a positive note, this brain tricking has helped me to keep fighting.

Something I learned from this: It's important that someone in the family asks the doctor to take the children to one side, away from both parents, and explain what has happened, and some of the behaviour they may experience. They are, after all, suddenly snatched from a child role and thrown into an adult one without any guidance from anywhere. Then at school they step back into role of pupil, otherwise they will be seen as being rude. Friends have since said that Henry went to their house after school sometimes, maybe stayed a night as previously. He was not having the friends over to our home, but otherwise he had not mentioned anything being different. If anyone asked how his mother was, he simply replied, 'Fine'. So they did not know I had had a stroke; was in the hospital, or any of what Henry was going through. It worries me he was struggling alone with the natural fear, denial, and anger.

As I've mentioned before, make sure you have a care plan in place before the stroke survivor leaves hospital. Ask for everything to be explained simply and clearly to you. Take as much time as you need to ask the hospital staff questions, they will not mind being asked. Be as prepared as you can be.

At first you will manage well but it will begin to take its toll so be careful. If you start feeling unwell that won't help any of you. If you become over tired that can lead to grumpiness, poor sleep and even depression. Friends and relatives all rally round in the initial stages and offer to help but with the person beginning to look visibly better their involvement may tail off as they return to their daily lives and you may find yourself coping on your own.

Advice for the Carer:
- Ask hospital staff to take any children aside separately and explain what is happening, encourage them to ask questions.

- Make sure you have all the questions answered before the survivor comes home.
- Make sure you have time out for you – hobbies, relaxation.
- Organise things for you and the child/children – normal activities away from the survivor, i.e., see a film, go swimming.
- Be honest about your emotions, you will be angry towards the survivor, it's natural.
- Make sure you and the children have someone qualified to talk to, don't cope alone.
- There is regular help for the survivor, but not you, make sure you get some.

Chapter Nine

Being the Carer

'Success consists of going from failure to failure
without loss of enthusiasm.'
Winston Churchill

The Carer's Experience – by Nick Edwards

There are two major challenges to coping as a carer of a stroke survivor, the physical disability which can be seen, and the emotional change which can't.

The physical disability is the easy one, the emotional is much harder and requires patience, strength, resolve, thick skin, understanding, and the ability to second guess what is needed/required at all times.

I can remember the day of Sas's first stroke as if it was yesterday. I was watching Henry play rugby at school when I had a phone call from her to say that everything was all right, but could I come to collect her from the doctors' office and take her to the hospital in Worcester.

When we arrived at the doctors' office, Sas was walking out. She got in the car and off we went to the hospital as if it was a regular occurrence. I didn't question how she got to the doctors', where her car was, but I do remember asking how she was feeling, to which the response was, 'Had a bit of a headache this morning and the doctor wants me to go in to hospital for a check-up'.

We arrived at the hospital and they were prepared for our arrival as Sas was whisked off for examinations and tests. The hospital staff kept Henry and I up to date with what was happening and soon it became apparent that they felt Sas had had a stroke, but didn't know the extent.

This of course meant nothing to Henry or I, we were oblivious to the fact that what had happened to the person we loved would change all our lives, possibly forever.

I cannot speak for Henry, but I was ill prepared for what was to come, possibly from ignorance, possibly from disbelief, but I think he felt the same.

My one major regret is that while all this was happening and I was wrapped up in my own feelings, I was unaware of how this was affecting Henry. He seemed matter-of-fact about it all, came to see his mum in the hospital on all occasions, said all the right things while there, but never expressed how he was feeling. I hope my indifference to his feelings has not scarred him for life.

The next time I remember seeing her was on the ward and it was a bit of a shock to say the least. It wasn't the same person I had brought in. Her face had dropped on one side, her speech was incoherent, and that was what I could see, heaven knows what the damage was I couldn't.

The doctors and nurses did their best to inform and reassure, but it wasn't enough to prepare me for the reality of what had happened and the enormity of what was in front of us all.

Over time it started to sink in, but I am sure that half of me didn't believe or didn't want to believe what I was being told. I couldn't understand how something like this could happen to someone so young, fit and healthy. I just wanted things to go back to the way they were and have my 'old' Sas back, and being selfish, get my own life back to what it had been.

One of the most difficult things for me to cope with was having to explain to others what had happened when they asked. I found myself getting very emotional and fighting back the tears as I tried to explain. If they didn't ask I would never bring it up. Even after three years it still makes me feel that way.

The following few weeks, while Sas was in hospital were exhausting. Trying to keep two jobs going, getting Henry to and from school, cooking, hospital visits every day, etc, but safe in the knowledge that Sas was in good hands and her care was being looked after.

I was still frightened and daunted about what was to come, there were so many unanswered questions. It was taking a lot of dedicated people to make sure that Sas was comfortable, bathed, washed, fed, and tableted. How on earth was I supposed to cope on my own while still having my other commitments? Even then, I was aware that the good intentions and help from others at home would soon disappear and that Henry and I would be on our own.

Seeing someone in the hospital does not prepare you for when they return home. Not knowing the limitations of the conditions, what can she do, what will she be able to do in the future and when, what facilities/adaptions are available and how will they help? Looking back I realise, selfishly, I probably wasn't looking forward to having her home, as I didn't know how or if I could cope, or who to go to for help.

When Sas finally came home, we were swamped with wonderful help from all, friends, family, and professionals who were used to what was needed. Our house had been turned into a home for the disabled, with gadgets, contraptions, things on toilets, things around basins, special seats, and commodes in the bedroom. We were told what we would be eating and when; I felt in the way with all the helpers. Don't get me wrong, I am so grateful for all the care Sas received during this time; without it she couldn't have been home and I wouldn't have been able to come to terms with what had happened.

Sas's stroke was something I couldn't see as there were no visual signs that were evident to me. Okay, a slight drop to one side of her face, but that faded, and some difficulty walking. I was ill prepared for the mental damage that had occured and the repercussions, memory, emotional (not being able to do what she had always done) blame (was it my fault?).
But I was starting to realise that my life was about to change even more once all the fabulous care and help stopped, from being looked after myself

87

by Sas, to looking after her totally. This means everything: getting in and out of bed, up and down the stairs, on and off the toilet, washing, bathing, dressing, cooking, feeding, plus trying to keep a full time job. My colleagues at work were great, giving all the support I needed to be able to concentrate on the most important thing, Sas's well-being. It didn't stop me from worrying about was she alright? Did she need to go to the toilet? I was fully aware that Sas remained in the bedroom until I could get home to carry her down the stairs but even then she'd remain in the same room in the same chair on her own for hours at a time. That was having an effect on her mental state that I hadn't realised or understood, but should have done something about.

The worry and stress was taking its toll on me, I was unable to concentrate, I was becoming irritable, shouting at Sas and Henry for no reason, driving too fast to get home just in case, losing weight through not eating, seeing requests as criticism, and trying not to lay the blame where it shouldn't belong.

I found the most difficult thing to come to terms with was that just because I could remember saying something or an event, Sas couldn't, and we had and still have disagreements about our recollections. She puts it down to her stroke, me to senior moments. Sometimes I just have to accept that she is always right unless she accepts she isn't.

I was still unsure of the effect all this was having on Henry, but he was always very supportive and considerate. Although having said that, he was a typical teenager, doesn't do tidying, cooking, washing up, or anything that involves housework, but I still loved him for just being there for me.

I had many offers of help from close friends, new friends and people I hardly knew, but turned many of them down. I knew that they were real and given from the heart, not just offers that people make because of the situation. But I also knew that if I accepted them I was only putting off the inevitable. I would have to cope sometime and it may as well be now. I couldn't let myself rely on others, as it wouldn't last, for they had lives too.

I was at home when Sas had her second stroke and fortunately so was a friend and professional occupational therapist, who knew what was happening and what to do. I also recognised the symptoms and realised it was about to happen again and that it could be fatal.

This time both Henry and I were more prepared, but that didn't make it any easier to handle; if we thought that last time was bad, this could be a lot worse. Thankfully it wasn't, my greatest fear wasn't realised.

One of the most difficult things that I had to cope with was coming to terms with changes in behaviour and personality. Sas was, at that time, not the same person that I had fallen in love with, had spent the last years with and who was my best friend. I was used to looking after the three of us, now all my efforts were focused on one person, Sas. I was neglecting looking after Henry the way I should and I also wasn't looking after myself. I found myself thinking that if I did, I wouldn't be capable of looking after others, but that is easier said than done as the initial 24/7 care just doesn't give you the time.

Things began to improve, mainly because of the determination, tenacity and drive that Sas had to prove everyone wrong who said that she'd never get any better. She became a little more mobile and independent thanks to all the efforts she and others were putting into her recovery. There were still things that I found difficult. Initially I could never understand why, when she was talking to people, she'd always tell them that she has had a stroke and always owned it. It was 'my stroke' not 'the stroke' or "a stroke". I guess it was her way of coming to terms with what had happened and seeing herself as a survivor not a victim.

Things I have learned:
Strokes can cause changes in someone's behaviour or personality. They may become impatient and irritable or withdrawn and introspective. Sometimes previous character traits can be reversed, with a mild-mannered person becoming aggressive, a difficult person becoming more passive, or a once sociable and lively person becoming withdrawn.

More commonly, however, existing traits are exaggerated. It can happen with many neurological conditions and often happens after a stroke that some become more emotional or have difficulty controlling their emotions. Some people describe the feeling as though all their emotions are 'much nearer the surface' or stronger after their stroke. For example, some people may become upset more easily, or cry at things they would not have cried at before their stroke. Their emotional response is in line with their feelings, but is much greater than before the stroke. For other people the symptoms can be more exaggerated, and some people find that they cry for little or no reason. Less commonly, people laugh rather than cry, but again the emotion is out of place and does not match how they are actually feeling at the time.

These emotions usually come and go very quickly, unlike when someone feels upset and is crying. Some people may even swing from crying to laughing. Although the individual realises that their crying or laughter doesn't fit the situation, they cannot control it and this can be very upsetting. These episodes of crying can often be misinterpreted as depression. Sometimes people with emotional liability have depression as well, but crying because of emotional liability is not necessarily a sign of depression. If there are doubts about whether or not the individual has depression, a mental health professional might be able to help by assessing and advising on treatments.

Family and friends of stroke survivors who are affected in this way often find changes to behaviour and personality hard to deal with. People can be upset by the things their relative says to them and may find them very difficult to live with or to be around. This is especially true if the stroke survivor becomes aggressive. If your partner, friend or family member becomes aggressive (in a way that you find threatening), it is important to remember that, despite the stroke, it can be quite frightening.

Some people find that the challenging behaviour is aimed only at them, and that the person affected by the stroke is reasonable with other people. This is really quite consistent with people's behaviour generally. Most of us more easily get cross with the people we are actually closest to, as we feel safe in the knowledge that they will probably forgive us and still want to see us. Some stroke survivors seem unable to recognise or understand that their behaviour or personality has been altered, and feel that there is nothing wrong with them, so they have no reason to change. This kind of situation is harder to manage, so it is important to get support from other members of your family as well. You may also find it helpful to avoid confrontational situations and to walk away if a situation is becoming too difficult to manage.

Some Advice:
As a carer, your well-being is important, for you as well as for the person you care for, look after yourself.

Carers get very tired, they don't sleep enough and they may do a lot of driving around, lifting, and cooking, which all can take its toll. The combination of psychological and physical tiredness can push people to the limits of their patience. Your own tiredness and depression may become bigger problems. Taking regular breaks and having time to yourself is crucial. This may be a few hours every day, or more formal respite care which can be:
- care in the home from a trained assistant
- care outside the home, such as at a day centre
- longer breaks, from a few days to a couple of weeks
Try to organise the day so that you have at least a little time to yourself. Ask family or friends for help with specific tasks.
One of my most important lessons I have learned but have not yet been able to put in to practice is, 'Don't think you have to do everything'. I have found it's much easier, quicker and with less upheaval to do it for Sas, rather than say, 'I'm sure you could do that yourself'. She is very capable of doing things when I'm not there; I mustn't take away her independence by trying to do

everything. If writing this has done anything for me it's that I need to learn the lessons and put into practice what I preach.

My Son's Experience – by Henry Wright

I was not even 16 years old and had gone for what I thought would be a normal day at school. I was playing in a rugby match which dad was watching when he had the phone call that changed our lives.

Everything was such a shock; so much to try and understand and take in as it all happened so quickly and no one was explaining anything to us.

I just remember dad and I having to have such long days. I got into trouble for being at school too early, but it was the only way dad could get to work on time. We had to go to the hospital every night, but I still didn't know exactly what to expect or how long it would go on for. I didn't fully understand that it would be a long term effect and the seriousness of it. Everything revolved around hospital times and our days seemed to be run by others. Every night dad and I would visit my mum and we'd spend hours talking to her about different activities I had taken part in, or how my day had been. It felt as if I would never get my mum back from the hospital, or ever see the day we'd finally bring her home. Every day was long but there still didn't seem to be enough time to get my tasks done as the majority of time was spent travelling. It turned into a routine of get up go to school, visit my mum, then start again. Although I was always tired and struggled to concentrate, at times I just thought how it must be worse for dad as he had to drive us everywhere, work, pay bills and stay strong for us, which is an enormous amount of pressure.

I didn't talk to anyone, even my closest friends, because I didn't know what to say, and I felt by talking about the situation it would look like I was trying to get sympathy, or people may treat me differently by just being overly kind. I also felt by not telling people and not being asked questions I could almost forget about it for a couple of hours and just try and be myself and the person my friends got to know. I used to think of excuses why people couldn't come over, or why my mum wasn't at home if they did visit.

Often I spent time at a friend's house. Jack and my "other mum" Kay were very supportive with the whole situation and respected my privacy with the situation but still ensured I was okay within myself. Kay was standing next to dad when he found out what had happened to mum so she knew as soon as we did. Kay used to collect me from school; take Jack and me to rugby matches, and gave me some normality back in my life. When another family friend (Louise) found out about mum's situation they also had me stay with them and I used to go to cricket with Sam. These kind actions and memories always stay with me and show
how special and supportive our friends are.

Our home was more like a hospital day by day as we had to make alterations to suit my mum so she could do a few of the basics. We had a variety of things fitted such as rails, things around the toilets, at the basin, in the shower, everywhere you looked. When people came over they would often ask about these different aids or we'd have to move them, which sometimes made us feel a little embarrassed. My mum had to be lifted out of bed, washed, dressed and then when she had eaten breakfast she'd fall asleep again. This was not the mum I had known all my life, dad and I had to lift her upstairs to bed and after school we'd have to rush home because she'd be in the chair where the nurses had left her until we returned; waiting to be taken to the bathroom. As soon as one thing went wrong it felt as if everything went from bad to worse, dad got pulled over for speeding as he was stressed and not paying attention. This then made him feel worse as he was worried about being delayed to get home and help my mum. It was clear dad was tired and getting unwell, but he wouldn't admit this and just carried on with his long days. Dad would be lucky if he had 6 hours sleep a night as he'd start work at 5 or 6 before he had to help my mum and take me to school. It's been hard getting used to mum's mood swings as she feels she has let us down and then gets cross with herself and sometimes takes it out on dad.

Not only do I worry about mum having another stroke but I also worry in case I have one, since people have told me it can be hereditary. However, mum reassures me that although her father has had a stroke, they were slightly different. His was a bleed and hers were both clots, so technically different conditions. Providing I have a balanced active healthy lifestyle I believe I will reduce any risk of health related illnesses.

I now realise that at different times we've all been acting strong to protect each other and in reality this is not healthy for any of us. The healthiest and kindest thing for everyone thrown into this situation is to talk to one another, and to be honest with each other. Everyone will feel the same at some point, but I have realised it is important to let others know you are there for them if they need help, but otherwise you must act as normal. I felt when I kept asking dad if he was okay it made things more stressful for him because it was a reminder of what had happened; so I'd let him know I was there for him but I wouldn't keep asking the exact same question: 'Are you okay?' This all happened so quickly without warning but we stuck together and dad has been amazing in the way he coped with it all and took control of the situation as much as possible. Throughout these past few years I look up to my mum even more because she is an inspiration in the way she'd never give up and always said she'd prove doctors wrong. Every time people ask me about her, they say how amazing she is that she hasn't let it beat her.

I miss not being able to play in the garden and do different activities with my mum but we still have such good fun and we have started joking about the situation, which makes me feel better. We can almost laugh about it as then it feels like we have beaten the stroke. When I take my mum swimming I have to put her in the pool but we even have a laugh doing that as I carefully throw her in, and then pretend I will leave her there. So although our lives have been suddenly changed we have not let this change our fun relationship, and she is still a brilliant mum to me. I know she often feels as if she has let me down but she has done far from this as I am proud I have such a strong mum. She hasn't let this stop her taking part in activities, she has recently started painting with her less dominant hand as it is the only one she can use. Mum picked up her hidden talent very quickly and has even sold several paintings for charity and others have been bought around the world. I almost think if it wasn't for the stroke she wouldn't have discovered these new skills. As hard as things get at times I say to myself that everything happens for a reason, and I believe this has made me a stronger person and my mum is still making the most of things she can do.

Another Carer's Experience – by Marie Bonnick

The role of carer for a stroke patient is a very complex one. It is often a husband or wife, a partner, a son or a daughter, who suffers a stroke and therefore it is a very emotional time as well as a worrying situation.

Sometimes one is aware that the relative is not well, but the signs are insufficient for the medical people to take notice. So there is the worry preceding the stroke. At other times a stroke occurs quickly and the shock is great.

The immediate needs of the victim are paramount.

Once the stroke patient is hospitalised there is a feeling of relief that he/she is being cared for and hopefully being rehabilitated. Stroke Units are the places where all this takes place.

Then the practical problems arise for the carer.

Time management is a main factor – keeping the home running smoothly, fitting in the shopping and visiting the patient regularly.

Finances have to be coped with. For example, I had never paid the bills or dealt with the bank. It was quite a learning curve! Luckily the bank was very helpful.

Travelling takes up a lot of time and money – I had many miles to travel each day for months, mainly during the winter weather, which was tiring and at times scary. Making sure that the tank was filled with petrol and change was ready for the car parking added to the stress.

At this time all is focussed on the patient. It is often difficult to get information from the professionals about your loved one. The carer can feel very isolated.

Later on when the patient is ready to come home, there are adjustments to be made - to the home, to life, to the future.

The carer has all the needs of the patient to attend to, the day-to-day activities, sometimes a wheelchair to manipulate (no practice beforehand and lots of incidents occur), and the responsibility of ensuring the loved one's safety. A sense of humour is essential! One is also dealing with the mental attitude of the patient, who is struggling to come to terms with the situation.

At this time the carer is often lonely, inwardly upset or worried. There is a need for someone to talk to, to reassure you, to sympathise. This is when friends are needed.

Carers need to be consulted, educated and helped to take on the role which has been put upon them, in the interest of the patient and the carer.

Despite the difficulties of caring there is a positive reward when one knows that he/she has contributed to the well-being and recovery of the stroke victim. Most people need that continuing care in order to flourish and regain their independence.

I acknowledge the help and caring of the Evesham Stroke Unit in my husband's recovery and the Stroke Association, which gave me the initial advice I needed at a very difficult time. May they both flourish in the future.

Chapter Ten

Stroke Number Two

'Go back a little to leap further.'
John Clarke

As mentioned earlier, Jane had changed her shift one Friday, just by chance; she didn't usually work for that team in the afternoon, but on that particular day she did. The stroke was happening as she arrived. She had the ambulance there so quickly and travelled with me to the hospital. Following the second stroke I had ICT in twice a day, every day, for the following weeks. They even came at weekends and on Bank Holidays. As well as helping me to recover and be motivated it was a tremendous emotional support.

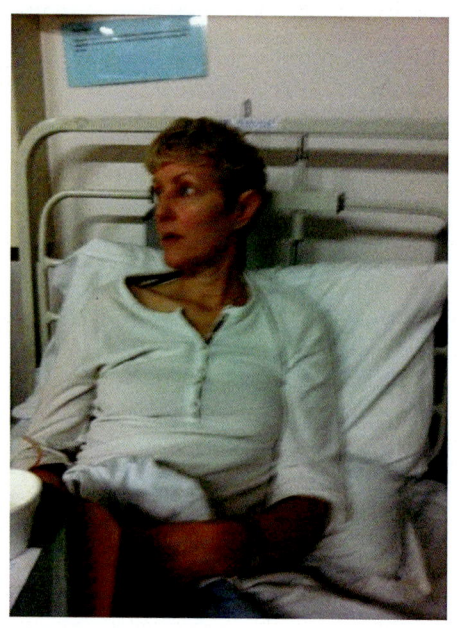

As you can imagine, I have looked back on that day many times. It started by doing all the right things. I had a long lie in as I still felt fatigued, and then had the usual breakfast tablet routine, hair washed and blow dried. I had then been sitting in the sun and as I went into the house to the cloakroom, I suddenly had a pain in my head, in just a small area, and then everything deteriorated. I do not actually remember Jane or the paramedics arriving. My first memory is in the ambulance with the blue light on and Jane saying she's so pleased she is strapped in, otherwise she would be flat on her face.

What this second stroke really brought home to me was the importance of getting medical help quickly. This time my visit to the hospital was different from the first in several ways. First, I had already been treated before arrival. This time people were expecting me and the Stroke Ward had familiar faces and routines with people saying, 'Hello, what are you doing back with us?' The following morning at breakfast there was no need to ask what I liked. Although I would rather not have been there, it was as friendly and comfortable as possible. Luckily, my friend and neighbour happened to be in the next bed which was company for both of us and also helpful for certain visitors who could sit in the middle of both of us and kill two birds with one stone, as visiting does take time out of their day.

The other fortunate thing was that my speech wasn't affected and everyone knew I wasn't going to shut up until I could be discharged. My argument about having the ICT team ready to start as soon as I returned home, which would free up a bed, won support fairly quickly, so there were no more stays in Rehab. The other reason I was desperate to return home was that Henry and his rugby team, along with parents, were all due to leave for France for a tournament, and I was determined to be on that coach. Kay and Michelle, two of the other mothers, were to be in charge of the wheelchair and determine where I would and wouldn't go; it was all planned. Needless to say, I didn't manage to go. My mother stayed with me and my friend Jacques took me to a French restaurant the night they left as my bit of the tour. Then, between sleeping, I watched films and I ate with my neighbours, Martha and Gerald and Sabine and Mike. I had my own tour of friends' dinner tables and a constant update of the rugby results and the state of the players and parents, so I still felt a part of it. Strokes do have a habit of ruining our plans but my message here is do not let it beat you and miss out on what can replace those things. Make the most of what we can do and we will still be able to have fun, even if only for a couple of hours before you fall asleep. That's fine. Just carry on when you wake up again.

My biggest lesson has been to learn to pace myself and not push myself so much. I sometimes wonder if that is why I had my second stroke, but I tell myself if it was going to happen it would have done so anyway. In a funny sort of way, as I sit here typing, I realise it has made me feel stronger. Having had one stroke you always wonder whether you will have another one and how you will cope while not yet having recovered from the first. Well, now I know, I am fine and feel that the fear has gone. Not only have I coped, I am now no worse off and that fear has been removed.

Complications You Could Encounter After a Stroke

Pain can be quite common following a stroke, often in the hip or shoulder on your weaker side. This is usually because of muscle weakness. It can be helped by deep tissue massage although it is quite uncomfortable at the time. It exercises your muscles to strengthen them. You can take pain relief but you are only masking the pain, you are not improving the situation.

Pressure Sores
These can happen when the person is bedridden for a while and their weight is on one area. They are painful and can be difficult to heal.

Cellulitis
This can be caused by simply banging a leg or by an insect bite but, if you don't have any sensation, you may not be aware. It can then lead to infection and get into your bloodstream and make you very unwell. You can be treated with antibiotics or you may have to go to hospital and have intravenous drugs.

Kidney Infection
I don't know whether we are prone to this because we are less mobile or because of medication. I had to be admitted to hospital because of this and was put on anti-nausea medication. I was unable to eat or drink for a while and had a high temperature. It all happened very quickly but took some time to clear.

Pericarditis

I have now experienced different illnesses that I had never even heard of. I had this ailment at the same time as my kidney infection, and it was a very strong pain in my chest. There was fluid around my heart and inflammation of the pericardium. This makes it very important for us to take extra care with our diet and exercise regime.

Nearly a Year On

By now, I'm sure you have many improvements to celebrate but, sadly, there are still more difficulties for you and your family to endure. This is what makes stroke such a quietly unkind, controlling condition. All this time, you have had to remain focused on improving, on getting well again. All the difficulties you have been presented with have made you even more determined. But, this is where the problems lie for both the stroke survivor and immediate family. That family feels almost worn down as the caring, loving person you knew has become selfish, self-focused on recovery and not able to see much beyond that. It is difficult for the patient because the limbs repair at a faster pace than the brain and people think you are back. In one way, this is what you have been waiting for; on the other hand, it is something you are unable to handle. People suddenly expect you to behave as you did before. You so much want to prove to them and yourself that you are back and that the old you has returned but it just isn't happening and you cannot cope.

This did happen to me. Things I would have done effortlessly before I tried to do again but they made me unwell. For instance, having my hair washed used to be a treat, but now my head felt like a wasps' nest, as if it was a mass of live nerves.

And when I tried to deal with things on the phone I still had to use my left hand and have the phone at my weaker ear. I had to concentrate so hard on the first part of the sentence that when the person talking to me had finished I only had a few words written on the paper. Without realising, my family felt let down because I hadn't achieved what I had meant to. Why? I always did, didn't I? And after all, I am back in appearance for the most part, so why am I not me, capable?

This is the stage when you hear many families say that their problems with depression begin. Friends and families think, 'Oh, they're better now, everything will be OK'. But although the person may look normal their behaviour isn't because their brain won't allow it. This is clearly worse for people who have never experienced any sort of disability before, and you hear them saying people don't understand how they feel and how they have lost their confidence. The brain simply no longer functions in the way that it did.

A prime example of this is a situation in which I found myself. Two people who came regularly to help me were causing me stress. A friend said, 'You need to tell them not to come anymore'. Once she'd said this, it was obvious, yet my brain couldn't arrive at that solution. Prior to us talking about it, I had been dreading every Thursday and worrying about how their behaviour and attitude towards me, would make me feel. I had lost the ability to process what was going on. The people we were paying to help with the chores I could no longer do, and reduce Nick's stress, were actually increasing my stress levels and making me unwell. Only those around me could really see what was going on.

Things to remember:

- pace yourself
- set realistic goals and carry them out
- keep believing in your full recoverably
- you need others to both help and give advice with activities

Chapter Eleven

A Year On – Rehabilitation DIY

'In order to succeed, your desire for success   should be greater than your fear of failure.'
Bill Cosby

Returning to Driving

Following a stroke you are not allowed to drive for a month and to be honest, I can't imagine that anyone would feel well enough or even be thinking of driving in the first few months. Even up to six months afterwards there are far too many other things to conquer.

Driving is something I have been longing to do right from the beginning. The thought of losing my licence was very upsetting, but I would recommend that you do inform the relevant authority, which in the UK is the Driver & Vehicle Licencing Authority (DVLA), of what has happened or get someone to do it on your behalf. They will send you a questionnaire for you to complete. If you have a problem with vision in one eye you can still drive but do need to be cleared by an ophthalmologist.

When the time is right, you can apply to the Regional Driving Assessment Centre (RDAC) and go along for an assessment and they will decide whether or not you will need some lessons. There are several in the country and my closest is Birmingham. Their frequency of appointments depends on where you live so, when you first phone, ask about the waiting time just in case it is long. The fee is £80 for a full assessment and test. Providing all goes well, they will give you a printout of the adaptations your car will need, all of which are easy to both fit and remove should you wish to re-sell the car. Some are very easy to remove such as the lollipop steering grip which just clicks off so that the car can be driven as normal.

You will also need to be able to go through the two-hour driving assessment, something which I still haven't managed. They then write a report and send both you and the DVLA a copy and your licence is either granted or revoked at this point. All through this process it is your safety and others' which is paramount.

Unfortunately, car insurance does become a little more expensive which feels like another kick in the ribs, but it does mean you are fully insured. The Stroke Association has a good contact for insurance.

A year on and I am still learning. I must admit that I fully expected to have started driving again by now and just as the 'old me' did, automatically, without even knowing I had done so. How wrong was I?

I went along for my first assessment which took about forty minutes, answering what would normally be primary school questions, in the car. My assessor had explained the adaptations I needed and we tried them out. That was an experience in itself – the unlearning and learning all at once. My brain was having a double chat with itself, part of it telling me to hold the steering wheel as I always had and to accelerate with my right foot, the other part also telling me I mustn't do that at all but must hold onto the funny control with my left hand and now use my left foot to both accelerate and brake.

I was there to impress this man that I could drive. I concentrated so hard. After this my brain was truly exhausted and I fought to stay awake while eating my lunch, and then fell into a deep sleep both before and after supper. I was like that for a week and a half.

The end result was that I had to have lessons and return when ready to sit a two-hour assessment. Due to bad weather conditions some time elapsed before I was able to have my first lesson and then I only managed 40 minutes after which I was no longer safe to be on the road.

The assessor identified that it was difficult for me to maintain concentration; if something caught my eye, my attention was diverted and I couldn't concentrate on two things, so I forgot I was in control of the car; my brain had shut down. The moment my lesson was over and I got into our car I fell asleep. I slept the remainder of the day and all of the following day apart from mealtimes.

My instructor was happy for me to continue but at a slow level. But, having spoken to someone at the Assessment Centre, it was decided that it was really too soon for me. I didn't want to experience yet another blow and I was so stubborn that I still booked my lesson for the following week. But I couldn't go to sleep immediately afterwards because this was when Nick had mistakenly put regular petrol into our diesel car, and I wasn't allowed to sleep in it until it had been sorted out, due to health and safety regulations. I had to go and sit somewhere and force myself to stay awake. Eventually it was fixed and I fell asleep on the journey home, slept before supper and then, just walking to the bathroom, I nearly collapsed. I had a tremendous pain in my head and felt unwell for several days. Finally, I listened to my body and cancelled the next lesson. My brain was struggling so much which was why it was shutting off and demanding sleep. I had been so determined to resume driving that I hadn't listened to my body's warnings.

I will drive again but not at the moment. It is now nearly two years since my first stroke and I have had my licence taken away from me permanently. I am truly saddened by this as it is not at all the result that I wanted, but I won't give up and intend to get back behind the wheel one day when I'm considered mentally safe. Meanwhile, I can assist in getting some of you back out there before me. Learn from my mistake – don't try too soon.

I have also found it very difficult as my son approaches his seventeenth birthday and he will be beginning his driving lessons. It would be natural for me to collect him from college or friends' homes and for him to practise driving with me at his side. Now, some of you may say I am fortunate by being saved the bother of teaching a teenager the rules of the road, but I feel saddened by this. As a mother it is one of those 'firsts', something that you expect to be able to help with. I can sit in the car but only with another adult doing my job; I cannot be the one sitting in the passenger seat as I no longer have a licence. This is one of the hardest things for me to deal with during this road of recovery.

Horse Riding – A Bittersweet Pill

I used to ride horses, so recently, I have started lessons with Riding for the Disabled. I need one-to-one sessions because I still have difficulties with concentration if there are other extraneous noises. But, you may find group exercises more enjoyable.

If you have ridden previously, do vet the riding school first. I speak from experience. They might say that they cater for your needs but, as I will explain, on one occasion I found otherwise and left feeling very hurt.

Riding may not be something you are drawn towards but is particularly beneficial to stroke survivors as it aids in the recovery of balance and some stability. The walking action of the horse stimulates the core muscles, which is something we may be unable to do at the moment. Consider giving it a try and, at the end of the day, it is only half an hour out of your week and you don't have to go back. I feel that if you have never ridden before it may give you a tremendous feeling of satisfaction, of escaping the rehab world and doing something 'normal', whatever normal is these days. It makes you feel an active participant. You will feel very tired afterwards and perhaps very sore and ask yourself 'Why am I doing this?' But, remember, no pain, no gain!

For those of us who have lived and breathed horses it is a different matter; it is an emotional roller coaster. I will express different feelings on different days – it has been bittersweet. It is a cruel reminder of who you used to be, what you used to be able to share with these magnificent animals. It reminds you of the freedom of open space, being out in the elements, the speed and the sense of danger. Now, here you are in an indoor school having been lifted onto an old cob who doesn't even want to walk unless forced to, and doesn't blink without being given permission first! Somehow, even the smell you loved is different. You can't go and catch them, fling your arms around them and groom all the mud off, things which perhaps weren't once on your list of favourites. No more mucking out the stables and fields and putting out the feed. Now, for half an hour a week, you simply feel like a bundle on something which, no disrespect, you wouldn't have entertained riding previously. It is cruel; it tears you apart. On a better day I feel strong enough to see it in a different light and as a really significant stepping stone.

It is strange to do something you were once so familiar with in such a different way, but it is a step in the right direction and it may bring me close to riding my horse Maddy again in the future.

Once more it depends on how people relate to you. I had one lesson with someone who was so patronising that if I could have got off and walked away I would have done so. I left feeling that I didn't care if I ever got on a horse again.

My first experience had been fantastic and I joked with my physiotherapist that, at last, I was leaving my kitchen! I was helped into my jodhpurs still wearing my Function Electronic Stimulation machine (FES) but, wow, it felt good and off I went into the outside world. We arrived and I met my horse, Billy. Poor Billy couldn't help being a cob and he was still a lovely fellow; but I love thoroughbreds, flighty, handful types! I was quickly reminded of my situation and we continued. The girl giving my lesson was excellent and she realised that I had ridden a lot previously and knew that I would soon be very bored if we remained in the indoor school, so she volunteered to take me out on hacks as soon as possible, walking by my side with me now obviously on a lead rope. I left feeling very tired, with my ligaments screaming at having been stretched, but so happy. I had taken part in something a little normal and we had a plan to continue.

Then I had a second stroke and a lot of time elapsed before I could return. When we did so the girl who helped me before was off for six weeks after a foot operation so a very different experience began.

I was told by this new woman to get on. I don't know her name so for the purpose of the story, let's laughingly call her 'Empathy'. 'Get on,' Empathy demanded as if I had somehow inconvenienced her. I couldn't find any words to reply, nor could my friend. She repeated her command and my friend replied, 'This is a disabled lesson, you are meant to put her on and then wait until the ligaments have settled before moving. Can we change the stirrup lengths?' Empathy huffed at this and Jan got me on with the use of a stick, FES, and block. Luckily, she is both medical and horsey which helped

and always finds a way when there isn't one. As soon as I was in the saddle, Empathy barked, 'Move, another lesson is coming in and they need the block'.

Well, minutes later, a little girl was weaving all over the school and knocking poles over throughout the centre. Her instructor's voice was filling the air and by now my brain had been completely scrambled. All during my lesson, Empathy could only manage the words, 'Pat Billy' and 'sit up straight'. I reminded her that if I didn't keep looking down at my foot and leg to see if they were still there I had no idea if they were or not. In reality, goodness

114

knows where I thought they had gone, but that was not the point. As my mind was not functioning in a logical manner at that moment I had to check.

Then she said, 'Look between his ears,' and oh, again, 'Pat Billy'. *Pat Billy?* I thought what the hell has he done to warrant a pat? He's only putting one leg in front of the other, admittedly more than I am capable of unaided. What about the pain I was experiencing, my hips being stretched apart, an action they appear to have forgotten how to master, this previously simple action now literally bringing tears to my eyes. So if she thought Billy needed praise I didn't share that with her. I felt my blood beginning to boil and just willed myself to be able to get off and walk straight to Jan's car. Empathy wouldn't even have noticed, to be honest, and they had my money. She made me feel completely useless, as if I wasn't worth bothering with. I left feeling if I never got on another horse again it wouldn't be too soon; I was close to tears. I still carry this feeling.

On the way home, Jan asked if I had been to the other riding school which we usually drove past. I explained that when the hospital phoned them for me they said they only did lessons for disabled children. She suggested that we call in anyway and ask if they would reconsider. I had mentally hung up my hat by then but just went along with it anyway.

We stopped by and asked them and they said they had recently started offering help to adults and they would be more than happy to help me. I asked for an anorexic horse as my hip was still very painful. They said that as I'd ridden before I probably wouldn't want a plodder so they had just the right horse in mind as he was narrow. Already things were looking up. Well, they were so friendly and so understanding of my situation; they treated me as though I was still a human being and asked me what my ultimate goal was. My situation was completely turned round and they did have a spare place in two weeks' time. The way I was feeling at the time, I wouldn't have minded if they had said two years, but we booked it anyway.

When the day came it was another pick me up. Three people helped me on to my horse, Spencer. One girl took control of the lunge so the instructor was freed up to walk round and check my body from every angle to see what was happening. We also talked about my long-term plans.

This was to be able to ride Maddy again; she is lovely but strong-willed and far from predictable and enjoys having just two feet on the ground. If I couldn't do that then I would close the door on riding.

Pre-Stroke

My instructor made the half-hour interesting and I came away feeling that I had actually achieved something, and Jan saw me actually laughing. The instructor had put poles down and I took Spencer in between them, admittedly at the end of a lunge which acted as a security blanket. She showed me how to hold the reins with my good side, but also putting the weak side on them. It was far from pretty but those days are a long way off.

I explained how Maddy and Rose, the horses I would normally have ridden pre-stroke days, needed to go out and I wanted to go out riding too. The instructor said that when I can handle the handlebar style of control we could go out for hacks on the common. If I don't succeed and I end up saying goodbye to riding, at least it will have taken me farther along the road to recovery and I won't look back regretfully wishing that I had tried. It is better to have tried and failed than never to have tried at all.

At this stage I don't see myself riding again. I am not yet saying that it is forever but it could well be. I'm not getting any enjoyment out of it; I just sit there having the constant longing to ride as I used to, and it is upsetting and I'm paying to be upset. It is a difficult enough road without taking on extra things which upset us, but I do recommend it for people who have never ridden before.

Swimming

If you don't fancy riding, try swimming. I feel this is a very beneficial part of our recovery process.

If you have a local hydro pool close to you all the better as you can take full advantage of its facilities and equipment, and it will also be lovely and warm and therefore really enjoyable. If not, like me, find a local pool that has disabled access, with steps or a hoist into the pool itself. It is better if it is small and shallow enough to stand up in – all the things we didn't like when we used to swim serious lengths.

Make sure you have a woggle which will become your best friend when you're in the water as your stick is when you are walking. When you use a woggle, you can practise some of the exercises you would usually do with your physiotherapist if the pool is empty enough and you feel sufficiently confident. If you put the woggle underneath your armpits you are safe, it won't go anywhere and it will keep you afloat. Using your strong side you can begin breast stroke movements and, as much as possible, try and mirror this with your weak side. The satisfaction you will have as you travel through the water will override the pain. Even if it is the strength of your non-affected limbs which are moving you up and down, you are increasing and encouraging movement, and you are telling your brain that you are moving both sides. All of this is good exercise and aids recovery. I promise you. Confidence also increases with each visit and people will begin chatting with you and, what's more, after a while they will notice small improvements which maybe you haven't; and this is all great motivation and also builds up your self-confidence. You will be tired afterwards so don't stay in too long. I felt I couldn't manage the showers there, as my stick would slip, so I just dried off and waited until I could be lifted into the bath at home; not ideal but preferable to falling. Being tired is fine as you have achieved something good. So, allow yourself a drink or something to eat if you feel hungry, and have a rest; you deserve it.

Things to remember:

- pick up a previous hobby/activity providing it still helps you
- swimming helps the recovery process and confidence
- horse riding helps core stability
- do not start driving too early and ruin your long term chance

Chapter Twelve

A Brick Wall

'The only way of finding the limits of the possible is by going beyond them into the impossible.'
Arthur C. Clarke

Fifteen months after my second stroke, everything took a turn for the worse on the emotional front. I had been drifting along for the previous few months although I was aware that a series of events had meant I'd been subconsciously battling with various emotions. But, wow! Suddenly they came tumbling down and my strength left me overnight; and the following morning I woke as a miserable wreck. That veil of depression that I had so cleverly avoided for over a year smothered me and the emotional pressures of recent weeks took over.

I had visited a specialist the previous day and she was as lovely as ever. But a few simple words indicating that this was how I would be for the rest of my life propelled me into an emotional dive; all my belief in myself and the power of recovery left me. My experiences with driving and riding had taken their toll. I only had to look at Maddy in the field and I couldn't hold back the tears. What had happened to me? I am someone who was always so active and now my days were spent sitting, eating and sleeping. My independence had gone. Walking outside was impossible in case I was knocked over by an energetic dog; I felt a prisoner in my own home.

Yet so much time had passed that people had begun to question me. I looked better but I still couldn't just hop in my car and go where I wanted; I had to be taken. They thought I should be capable of more. People say they will pop in but they don't and you just carry on sitting in your home, day in and day out, bottling everything up and feeling sad.

Hang on! There was meant to be a lesson here about how to look after myself and my feelings. Would I never learn? Was I slipping back into old ways? Having put in so much hard work I couldn't let this happen. I decided to allow myself a few days to do whatever it took to let the tears flow and talk to my friends. I said, 'I WILL NOT BE BEATEN. I AM GOING TO GET BETTER'. Just having a night's sleep would be a blessing without any pain or headaches.

The following day, my physio discovered some of the causes of my pain. When I had had my stroke my arm and leg twisted so much that it pulled two bones out of line which had since been rubbing together. These, in turn, caused a knock-on effect on adjacent muscles and ligaments which manipulation could ease. But the reason and logic didn't appease my stress. The specialist had told me to keep an eye on feelings of depression as they do go hand-in-hand with stroke, especially where there is paralysis. Saying that pressed another button telling me that here was yet another thing to deal with.

I knew it had hit me when we travelled down to our holiday home in Cornwall. I love it there but, this time, I didn't even want to go. I loved it, but there I was refusing it. It was as if my heart hadn't joined me. I didn't feel like visiting any of our favourite places. I couldn't shake the feelings off. Nick bought me my favourite drink, champagne, but that didn't work; I didn't want it. Again, I loved it but there I was, refusing it. I had a few days like this, not tearful, just low and completely flat with no fight in me.

And then I felt I had to turn it around. I thought maybe I had to go this low to realise that I hadn't made any progress for a long time, and that in my late forties this is how I would be for the rest of my life. I just couldn't bear the thought of that. If I hadn't been such an active person beforehand maybe I wouldn't have felt so desperate. Maybe this was the extra push I needed to make me fight harder? Driving was shelved, riding was emotionally crippling; I needed a new plan and workable goals to give me a purpose in life. Right then and there, if I didn't get up in the mornings it wouldn't actually make any difference to anybody. I needed to find a way to change that.

I realise now that I'd been aware that I'd reached a plateau, but it hadn't dawned on me that if I didn't do something more my recovery would stop. The heavy cloud that had smothered me was actually a blessing in disguise, a wake-up call to work even harder and ensure that the past year's struggles weren't wasted. As I write this I know everything is easier said than done. Emotional lows can't suddenly be lifted and it would be so easy to crawl back into a warm, cosy bed and think about it all tomorrow.

This is a time when you need someone by your side encouraging you, saying, 'You can do it, think how far you've come, you can push a little bit further.' Healthcare support should really be there for us. The more I talk to people at my Stroke Club the more it's clear that support is there for the first year and then there's nothing. That is exactly when we need more push to get us to go the final mile; without that we stay on a plateau.

So, I've devised a plan of action not only for myself but for anyone reading this book to adapt as required. In principle, I believe it can work for us all if we remember key factors:
- work hard when you can
- respect your brain when you need to
- sleep to keep the balance right
- do not overdo things or nothing will be gained

Personal Plan

I asked my physiotherapist to write a series of exercises for me. I would do these at home and they wouldn't cause me any damage. They would be tailor-made for me, and you can do the same in a daily/weekly routine and set up a personal timetable which recognises the limitations of transport, personal or public.

I decided to work a five-day week, from Monday to Friday, then weekends would be family time. It's up to you whether or not you put in any extra time, but it's really valuable to have the special time with your family. I also included a weekly massage which is very good for you, as I've mentioned before. Do your best to book the same day and time each week and get as deep a massage as you can to waken up your tissues and muscles. I had one last week and I felt that blood was flowing around my body for the first time in fifteen months. I felt completely energised, awake and pleased when it was over!

My physiotherapist suggested I buy an exercise ball which you can get from Argos online, to avoid shopping. They are not expensive and can really help you if you have somewhere flat outside or in your home.

You can also buy a folding Mirror Therapy Box off the Internet which improves recovery of arm function. You put your weak hand inside the box and do the exercises with your strong hand; your brain is easily tricked into believing you are doing the exercise with both hands and this therefore helps with the rewiring of your brain.

My exercises are:
- opening and closing my hand
- twisting my hand over so that the back is on the table, and back again
- bending and straightening my wrist
- touching each finger with my thumb
- reaching for an object
- gripping a cup then sliding my hand back again
- picking up pieces of pasta and putting them into a cup

It's advisable to do these for fifteen to twenty minutes twice a day. Get someone to write a programme with you, which is possible and attainable, and get it updated as you move along.

My physio wrote me a plan and I then asked a personal trainer to help me for one hour a week for two weeks to get me motivated and started. I also managed to book a lift at a local swimming pool three times a week so that I could go on my woggle up and down the pool trying to extend movement in my hip joint, strengthening my shoulder and increase the use of my arm.

The plan looked like this:

Monday – Exercise plan, a little swim then sleep
Tuesday – Stroke Club every other week, lunch then massage
Wednesday – Afternoon swim
Thursday – Exercise plan. (This could include the treadmill or mirror box)
Friday – Hospital in the morning, lunch, a rest then swimming

This way there is always room for a change but there is at least a structure and it stops you from drifting. There is a focus. If, one day, you just don't feel well enough, it doesn't matter; your body is telling you that it needs to rest. Just skip that day and start afresh the next. Don't beat yourself up about it; those days are over. It is tough enough without giving yourself a hard time.

Having said that, you do need to push yourself to a personal limit in order to achieve any benefit; not so that you feel unwell but you will know when you need to stop. If you hit an obstacle, think 'red alert!' and make sure you are still pushing forward. Visualise yourself fully recovered and keep this in your mind while exercising.

I now go on a running machine as I've damaged my knee and can't go swimming. OK, I need help to get on and off, it has to be turned on for me, I only walk but I can hold on to the bars for stability and I have to be supervised. I also have my FES so the natural buzz is fantastic because I am walking without my stick and I feel close to recovery. The surface is flat and safe so it increases my confidence as well. I started off very slowly and sought advice about changing speeds, distance and gradient and my aim is to walk three miles a day. Don't worry if you aren't still under a specialist or physiotherapist, you can be your own. I know in my head when it's time to stop and I have to go to sleep straightaway, but I feel great that I have achieved something. I also believe that the repeated actions send messages to my brain aiding my recovery so I'm getting the feel good factor and adrenaline.

I have half an hour twice a week with a personal trainer doing exercises for my arm and core muscles. I have to sit on an exercise ball while doing the arm exercises and then rest. When I'm able to increase this to an hour we will do this twice a week. I also find intermittently using my mirror box very helpful.

Remember two things – your needs will be slightly different, and I am not in any way medically trained; I am just a fellow stroke survivor sharing my experiences which might help you.

Something else that emerged as this fog of gloom began to clear was that I have spent all my life trying to please others; putting others first. Worrying always about what other people think of me and my efforts. This is in Eamonn's words: Time for my PSP (post stroke personality). How can I have forgotten already? I have to make a conscious decision to start caring about me and my feelings not that others think I should be better because of the time that has lapsed. Let go of the desire to please; resolve that problem, solve things, and realise the only thing that I can really control and that really matters is my attitude to my current condition/circumstances. My feelings. It's about placing myself in the right frame of mind so that I can feel good before I tackle my next challenge, be it answering the telephone, physio, or simply holding a conversation. Remaining positive. I know I will still have thoughts wishing I was allowed to drive and be independent but I simply need to let them in, give them attention, then think maybe in time I will drive again, but for now I have been given the gift of opportunity. This is something very few of us get, as a result of which, I have written this book which will hopefully help many; and I have learned to paint with my non-dominant left hand.

Prior to the stroke I couldn't even write a legible word with this hand. Anytime I feel negative thoughts creeping in I must remind myself of these things; the enjoyment I receive from my painting, how it has benefited me and to make sure I expand on feeling the good emotions. This is something I recommend strongly as an exercise for us all. We will have many negative times so to find a way out is so much better than remaining with negativity. Remember too these are only emotions, feelings, all external, just little bubbles of thought outside of our bodies, so we can address the ones that do not serve us well and let those bubbles float away. Breathe in the good feelings. At this point we can progress from a stronger place within.

Things to remember:

- conscious thought to start caring about you and your feelings
- let go of the desire to always please others
- every time you feel negative thoughts creeping in, replace with positive ones
- create a personal exercise plan

Chapter Thirteen

Hobbies

'Every artist was first an amateur.'
Ralf Waldo Emerson

It is very important that you find a hobby, something you can do when you are sitting on your own, and which gives you pleasure. This could be something familiar or entirely new. If you used to enjoy something before but now struggle with it because of your disability then I would recommend that you do something different. Otherwise you will feel frustrated with the constant reminder of what you used to be able to do rather than benefiting from the new hobby, as happened to me with riding. You could try painting or sewing, knitting, doing crosswords, game apps on an iPad, gardening, or playing a musical instrument. All of these can be done on your own at home. I'm sure you can think of others. A few people in my stroke group enjoy gardening and grow their own vegetables and find it very relaxing. It is important to do something else outside the recovery program which we can manage on our own without having to ask anyone for help. The benefits are endless.

Painting

I started painting, something I had never done before. I have to work with my left hand which is a new experience, but I do enjoy it and it helps me to relax and do something absorbing during my hours alone.

One day, at my local Stroke Club, a lady came along to give us a morning's painting opportunity. My first reaction was revulsion. 'I can't use my right hand enough to write, so how am I expected to use a paintbrush?' My left hand had just about mastered a spider's attempt at writing so that wasn't going to be a great deal better. I didn't want to appear rude or ungrateful so I grabbed a brush in my left hand and joined in with the others. Having nearly dipped my paintbrush into Jim's tea more times than the water it wasn't looking too good, he won't rush to sit next to me during such an activity at Stroke Club again, but then I began to get into it. There was no sense of competition and it didn't matter if I made a mess. Everything could be cleared up and my excuse for a masterpiece could go in the waste bin without anyone being any the wiser. So, I tried a little longer. To my amazement, at the end of the session, the lady insisted I take my work home along with two paintbrushes and have a go at home. I smiled politely thinking I must remember where I'd put the brushes so that I could return them at a suitable time.

Surprisingly, when I got home, Henry noticed my carrier bag and questioned who had done the painting, saying it was lovely. Well, obviously I thought he was humouring me until Nick walked in and said the same thing. This was the beginning of many enjoyable hours. Later, I was actually able to make a birthday gift voucher for a friend. This could be easily done on a computer but I preferred to do it by hand, as I'd always done, and I couldn't wait to present the gift. I needed something to copy and I wasn't able to get anything straight from my head but that didn't matter to me.

After one of my treatments, I asked Nick if we could call in at a shop and buy some cheap watercolours, a pad of watercolour paper and a mixing palette. Even better, the paints were on sale, so it just made my choice quick and easy.

A friend lent me two of her watercolours to copy and off I went. Half the time I don't have a clue what I'm doing, but I'm getting so much pleasure from my new hobby it doesn't matter. The feel good factor is also amazing  because I can do this completely on my own without the usual requests I have to keep on saying and hate so much these days: 'Please can you?' or 'Please will you do this for me?' There's none of that. I can do a picture from start to finish when I'm completely alone. Then, the icing on the cake is when people admire my work. I just try things as I go along. When I thought a colour looked a little dense, I put water on my brush, went over it, and then thought, 'now what?' So, I got some kitchen roll and dabbed bits off. I liked how it looked so I use this method quite a bit now.

I still only have the same two brushes and am actively using them rather than waiting for 'a suitable time' to return them. I'm just saying that if someone suggests trying something new, ignore the fear factor and go for it. You don't have to do it again if you didn't enjoy it but, if it has the same buzz for you and is therapeutic as painting has been for me, you won't look back.

If you think you might like to try painting, consider starting with acrylics. They are straightforward to use, dry quickly if you use them straight from the tube, and if you make a mistake you can just paint over them, even yellow over black! I find that because I'm using my left hand, not my dominant one, I'm painting slowly, which means that the paint dries on the palette before I want it to. I then have to mix more

and it's difficult to get the same colour twice. I didn't particularly enjoy acrylics at first but I'm persevering and won't let them get the better of me. They're quite different from watercolour paint when you can just add more water on the palette and refresh the colour you need. So, it needed a

different approach and practice and a few tips from my artist friend, Sue. You can purchase adaptive paintbrushes which are easy to grip and they're available online, so no problems having to get to the shops.

I have more recently moved onto oils which is a very forgiving medium, it allows you the luxury of time because it takes so long to dry you can return back to your work many times and paint over things you wish to change.

The downside is that the oils are more expensive and the lengthy drying process can take up to several months depending how thickly you have applied the paint.

Musical Instruments

This is a great therapy and enjoyment. Brain researchers are now discovering that music not only calms, stimulates and triggers elation; it also helps to heal. Findings by the Music and Neurological Function, a research centre in New York: Not only does music decrease agitation and stimulate memory in patients with dementia, but it helps stroke survivors recover the power of speech, strengthen muscle groups and increase range of motion in patients beyond the help of traditional rehabilitation. You can learn at home, so again you don't have the difficulties with transportation issues. Your iPad is a great companion here; it offers many apps that teach you the basics of playing the piano, guitar, or harmonica for instance. You can use headphones so no one else can hear if you feel more comfortable, and if you decide this is for you and would like to take it more seriously you can find a teacher who will come to your home to help you. Again this can offer such a sense of achievement; something that you didn't do prior to the stroke.

Playing drums is another excellent way to help stroke survivors to communicate and simultaneously aids muscle control and cognitive skills as well as being enjoyable. Also consider keeping rhythm while you listen to some of your favourite songs.

Singing

This has proven both beneficial and enjoyable to stroke survivors and all types of acquired brain Injury individuals. It has been shown to help in the return of speech. While relaxing and enjoying the song a person is not so focused and tense about their speech practice and more able to manage some words. There are special organisations that come to stroke groups and Headway to practise singing.

Research shows that people who suffer from aphasia, due to brain injury, can be helped by singing. Losing yourself in an enjoyable melody helps the words to flow. Many people who cannot speak can sing; by encouraging the brain you bypass the damaged area as they follow a melody and eventually create a new circuit which helps to get them talking again. This is known as Melodic Intonation Therapy. It involves getting people to repeat and sing words and phrases, and becomes even more fun when using your hands as would a conductor, altering the pitch of the words. This takes the pressure off the person concentrating on the actual words, rather the focus is on trying to sing high or low, and the results are generally good. It is thought to take seventy to eighty sessions to be effective so it takes time but it works. If you also get the person to tap with the left hand while singing this stimulates the brain as well. Although it is the left-hand side of the brain that is responsible for language, it is both sides which stimulate speech.

Breathing to a rhythm, for example, can relax you; making a sound with an elongated vowel causes the body to vibrate. Depending on the sound this then affects the pelvic area or the chest. This in itself can be a diversion from pain and at the same time an emotional release. Music and singing can both turn on verbal and visual pathways to a brain that cannot be accessed by other therapies, and you are enjoying yourself at the same time.

Writing

When I suggest this I'm not saying everyone should write a book. I'm encouraging you to keep your personal record of achievement and emotions, etc. Again, you may say you have enough to cope with just trying to get better but writing can be something that is very valuable and uplifting as you reflect on your efforts and progress. Or just jot down random thoughts. We forget what we could not do and merely look at what we still can't. On days when you are feeling sad and fed up with the world you can look through your notebook, or iPad, and remind yourself of the times when you could not get out of bed, get dressed, get out of a chair, have a conversation, make a drink, etc.; then look at what you can do now. Maybe record the first time you made a drink, had a wash unaided, and went into a room you previously couldn't get into. As I write this I still have not been into our shower room because it has two steps and nowhere to put a rail. Write when you first managed to get upstairs. You will realise just how well you

134

are doing and what a long way you have come and how many expectations you have exceeded. You could also include photographs as a record and will be able to see how you are beginning to look better and so much stronger.

Since I started writing this book, I've been doing more painting, encouraged by an experience I had in Cornwall quite recently. One summer we decided to go to Polperro for a couple of hours. It's a little fishing village Nick and I both love and have visited several times with friends and on our own. It was festival time and there was a lot of activity on the quayside. There were several people sitting painting squares which would eventually create a large mural. It was a fund-raising activity where locals and visitors paid money to copy, in acrylics, a small square of one of a local artists, Sue Lord's paintings of Polperro Harbour. These were then stuck onto a huge board and gradually the enlarged painting emerged. It sounded simple to the likes of Sue and her friends but for me it looked scary and impossible. I was happy

to just look on, watch others and then go off home via the Blue Peter, which is the pub just at the end of the quay.

But, no, Sue and Nick had other ideas. She very kindly offered to help me if I stayed and had a go. Help? I needed more than help, I needed a miracle! Well, I didn't want to sit next to the people who were already there, as lovely as I'm sure they were, they were far too talented and would make it impossible for me to switch off and convince myself I really wasn't doing this. Well, true to her word, Sue really helped me all the way through and Nick provided cups of coffee to warm me up a little; this was, after all, an English summer and cool. At the end of a very long time, I have no idea how long, I had a finished square, my little piece of Peak Rock, created with my left hand, in acrylics. It was all a completely new experience for me and under the watchful eye of a hugely talented artist and that was the really scary bit. I have to say that Sue could not have done more to help me and put me at ease. The three of us went to the board and velcroed my section of the rock to the mural. It sat with the squares of the real artists. I felt a mixture of exhaustion, disbelief, shock and pride. Nick took a photograph of it so when we returned to the lodge that evening I e-mailed it to my friend and neighbour, Sabine, telling her about my day.

Before leaving, Sue very kindly gave me her details and offered to help me further and that was the beginning of our friendship. Our visit to Polperro was far longer than intended and for me the whole time sitting on the quay was very special. It was a very big and successful event. Sue was interviewed by Radio Cornwall and the finished mural was given to the local primary school.

The day has long gone but I have a super friend as a result of the experience and a hobby I adore. I now paint in oils and having purchased and tried water colour and acrylics, I have found the medium I most enjoy and will stick with but it will be different for us all. I have shared some of my paintings in each medium with you and watercolour was my gateway to it all, and what has enabled me to fundraise for our local stroke group.

Months later, I asked Sue for her recollections. She said:
I was sitting on the quay with other friends from the Arts Foundation Gallery encouraging people to paint a square and at the same time raise some money to try and keep our gallery open. We were asking people of all ages

and abilities to be involved, to enjoy being creative and perhaps pick up a paintbrush for the first time since leaving school. The youngest turned out to be three years old and the oldest, eighty. It was cold but very absorbing. At one point I turned around and saw a couple watching intently. A bit later they were just behind us and seemed enthralled. I asked if they'd like to have go. Nick said no but he encouraged Sas to try. She quickly said she'd had a stroke and would have to use her left hand. I said that was fine, I was there to help. She was lovely, full of humour but very self-deprecating. We chatted a lot over several hours and gradually

137

conquered her nervousness, step-by-step. I had never taught anyone who had had a stroke so it was a completely new learning experience for me, and I willed her to paint something of which she would be really proud. Patient hours passed and the cold chilled us, but Sas really persevered and produced a lovely painting. She was exhausted yet so pleased and really felt a sense of fulfilment. I was thrilled for her especially when she stuck her square onto the mural, smiling with relief and happiness. Nick's eyes were shining too. It was a fantastic achievement for Sas and the whole project was worth doing just for her.'

Gardening

This is something that can provide an interest and at the same time have many benefits therapeutically. Just 30 minutes a day, gardening can aid recovery following a stroke. Sensory stimulation and improving cognitive skills are helped by horticultural therapy in people with brain injury. Survivors can use a system where they are guided as to what they are be able to plant. This not only provides enjoyment but builds brain function at the same time. It also provides a sense of achievement and that increases personal satisfaction and self-esteem. Another huge advantage is that often it takes the survivor outside, which in the summer exposes them to sunshine; producing a source of vitamin D. While taking part in this hobby the survivor is more active and doing physiotherapy in itself, and also using far more muscles than just sitting inside. This also helps in the prevention of conditions like diabetes by keeping active. You could simply work on an area in your garden to grow beautiful flowers to look at, or you could have a project where you grow your own vegetables and/or herbs, which will be even more satisfying and healthy. You could start off with a simple window box or potted plants on the patio and take it from there. You can buy adapted gardening tools for the disabled and there are charities to advise you with these.

Good Old-fashioned Games

Chess and checkers are games we have all come across in our lives but need a partner to play with; these days with the ever increasing emergence of clever electronic devices, such as mobile phone applications, we can now play against the computer or with others online. You can also use a large print version of Scrabble. These help pass the time and can be enjoyable, and again all help with our cognitive abilities. You can look on mastergames.com and find games for disabled people.

Living Comfort: Pets

Numerous research studies show that having a pet improves the feeling of well-being. A new dog or cat may simply be too much responsibility now, but there are other options open to you. One may be a dry aquarium.

This is an attractive and relaxing addition to a home, and is not difficult to maintain. You could possibly keep lizards or frogs or even Tarantulas. This is something that personally leaves me cold at the thought, but some people like these pets; such as hamsters, guinea pigs or rats, and even believe they are cuddly! A rabbit is another option. Whatever you chose it is because it's an interest to you, and you get pleasure in owning and looking after it. It is an interest and is something that needs you; something that is often missing for us in this new situation we find ourselves in.

A fish aquarium is also an option, but you may need help with both assembling it, and later cleaning the tank from time to time.

Capture and Keep it

Photography is something that many people get pleasure from. There are many courses available at local colleges for disabled people to do photography, so I recommend getting someone to enquire on your behalf. There are also many online photography projects you can join. You can find out more by looking at 365project.org, but basically you take a photograph a day every day for a year. There are many accessories for disabled photographers too, so you overcome the problem of struggling to hold heavy equipment.

Fitness

Just because we are disabled it doesn't mean we are unable to exercise. There are modified fitness classes at groups across the country; yoga, Pilates, Thai Chi, aerobics, and many more. Just going out for a short walk, or going for a swim, all help and make you feel better too. Or go to the gym. I admit we need help and it is limited what we are able to do, but remember it is possible. If it is in your budget, you can hire one of the gym's trainers to help you. You can also buy DVDs of chair-based exercise workouts, and exercises for specific health issues.

Personal Scrapbook

Buy a pretty and good quality scrapbook; possibly even decorate the cover to personalise it. Get someone to help you cut pictures out of magazines of things you used to love doing, or hope to do again in the future. Include photographs of things you have achieved already since returning home. These can be a window box you planted; a picture you painted for a friend, a photograph taken of you playing an instrument. Anything - but it is the beginning of a visual record. You can also include the ticket stubs from the first time you managed to travel on a train or a bus; visited a museum, or went to a cinema or a theatre. You could include tickets or photo memories of a fun day out to remind you that this may be something you'd like to do again. It becomes a personal pictorial record of things that are special to you and at the same time reminding you of things you have achieved and things you intend to achieve. If you feel a little low one day take this scrapbook out and lose yourself in reliving the happy memories you have collated within.

Cooking

This is something we all struggle with for the obvious reasons but we can also have fun with certain aspects of it. I joked about putting a book together called *The One-handed Chef*. I have found supper dishes that I can manage and enjoy doing with a little help from others or by using ready chopped products like onions, carrots, etc. Prior to my stroke I would never have purchased such things, considering them both lazy and overpriced, but needs must, and if it means you are still having home cooked food, fresh vegetables, and your family can return home to a prepared meal; where is the harm?

Another absolute blessing is my slow cooker as I can prepare the main part of the meal, a beef casserole for instance; then when Nick or Henry are home they can lift it out for me to serve, and either mashed potato or rice could have been prepared and added. It also means they come home to the welcoming smell of food.

Another favourite of ours is stir fry; again everything is prepared and ready. I just fry it up; add the sauces and noodles, and someone else serves it up for all of us.

I get such a tremendous sense of satisfaction too when I have been able to prepare the entire supper. My first ever achievement was Eton mess for friends. I had to think of a pudding I could manage one handed, so what better than Eton mess? I can't tell you how many times we have eaten and enjoyed it since! I have now progressed to Pavlova and recently had such fun with Henry and his girlfriend Beth making one too. I actually felt needed and useful as Beth asked me if I would show her how to make Pavlova; so I supervised something I haven't done since my stroke, and Beth created. She and Henry decorated it together. We had a fun time and a delicious pudding too; it didn't last very long. You can be far more adventurous than I am and get back to making cakes too, but remember always make sure someone else is home to help with lifting the food out of the oven. Another scary thing I still do even now is that I can put things in the oven, or on the hob, but I then forget they are there.

Flying

This is something which most of us take for granted. Following a stroke, so much time has elapsed before we can even entertain the thought of flying. As much as we would love a family holiday in the sun, it has not been an option for me until recently. I did ask my specialist if I would be able to attempt a flight now, and was pleased to hear that it was possible providing I had very good insurance, drank a lot of water, and moved as much as possible during the flight. My medication would also provide protection. This is just my personal advice and everyone's situation is different, so always discuss it with your specialist. I had mixed emotions; I was excited at the thought of us all managing a holiday for the first time in three years, yet nervous at the same time about flying and also being away from everything that is familiar. We discussed it half-heartedly but circumstances then made us consider it very seriously when Nick's younger brother, Michael, who lived in South Africa, died. The news came as a sudden shock as we only heard of him being ill a few days before. Nick now needed support, so all my emotions and concerns needed to be concealed. I didn't sleep for a few nights before the flight as every permutation of events was bouncing around in my head. This added to my pressure as I would never have forgiven myself if I became unwell and caused Nick to miss Michael's funeral, even though it was something I had no control over.

Once on the plane and about to taxi off there was an announcement informing us of complications having to do with the fuel. On rectifying this

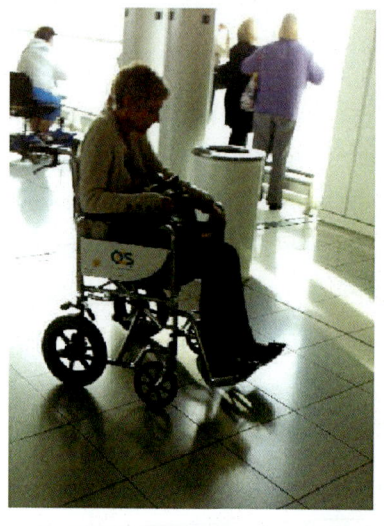 they had noticed a dent in the side of the aircraft which needed further inspection and our journey that night depended on their decision. Two hours passed and the plane was very hot and stuffy and people became agitated. The captain visited us all and tried to pacify people, but when there were no answers after two hours the atmosphere was not calm and quiet. This was not what I had hoped for on my first post-stroke flight and I was worried that we would arrive too late to attend the

funeral. However, I had to appear outwardly calm and not worried about time restraints. I did suggest trying to get off to see if there was another flight, but Nick preferred to stay, so we did. I tried to stop battling with thoughts in my head replacing them with ones I preferred – not an easy task. At last we heard good news and were asked to return to our seats as we had permission to take off. Apparently it was just a problem of paperwork.

Hidden Emotions

We must remain positive as it is our defence and our strongest tool in the box of recovery, but some days our mind plays the envy game. Envy of the life we had and the person we used to be. It can happen when we are with people who resemble what we used to be or who do things we most loved. You are longing to still be there but living in this body that just cannot. I find that summer is the hardest time to deal with this. Still being as excited as I have always been for friends as they buy their lovely holiday bikinis and dresses and sandals, go off jet skiing or simply walking into

Pre-Stroke

the sea for a swim, browsing at the shops at the airport before their holiday begins. Talking of all the dashing here, there, and everywhere that has to be done before they depart, checking messages, writing lists, fitting in last minute things, hopping into their cars looking super, tanned, fit, and moving with the ease you would expect in your forties, then driving off again. The independence that also goes with this age, and I sit and look on feeling like a great grandmother living in the wrong body somehow trying to hold onto this positivity I keep talking about. If I look through photographs of me riding or skiing or a similar sport I feel so detached yet longing. I almost feel as though I am someone who has died and is looking down at a flashback of my life, not that of course I would know what that was like, but it just feels so far away from me and so unattainable, yet I long for it.

145

Pre-Stroke

Oh, how I long to be active again and to be able to wear clothes and shoes I like, and feel feminine in, rather than those I am able to wear. Also when we go out, to just select what I fancy from the menu rather than, depending on the company, what I can manage with one hand. The funny thing is, as I write this I am not feeling low - quite the opposite in fact. I am doing something each day to improve and I attend an art class once a week which although I'm struggling with I enjoy. Although one week Sabine and I both sat in the car, looked at one another, and so nearly went to the pub instead. I was too fatigued and she had had a tiring day at work; however just as we were about to depart we had been spotted, so class it was! We made up for it when we returned home though I really did need a drink after that class, attempting to do life drawings using live models in a church hall pretending they were on a beach; and remember with my non dominant hand. At this stage I hadn't decided whether or not to include this drawing in the book, but I have since thought it beneficial to include to illustrate that literally anyone can have a go at

drawing and even enjoy it even when you have no prior experience.

146

Things to remember:

- remaining positive is our strongest tool to recovery
- find a hobby to fill the many hours we spend alone
- pets not only provide comfort but make us feel needed

Chapter Fourteen

Alternative Therapies and Treatments

'The power of the imagination makes us infinite.'
John Muir

These all have a place and have worked for me. On the other hand, it may be a chapter you choose to skip. It all goes back to choice and what works for you. However, you are not in a rush to go out and meet deadlines, and you want the maximum recovery, so I ask you to at least glance through this rather than feeling it isn't something you would be interested in. Again, it is the power of the mind.

Yoga

There are different forms of yoga originating from India hundreds of years ago. The one I have practised and believe to be beneficial is *Iyengar* yoga. It is gentle and as you progress into holding poses for greater lengths of time it stretches your muscles, aligns your body and frees the energy flowing through you. Practising your breathing can help your recovery and increase your sense of well-being and calm, reducing your anxiety and stress level.

Pre-Stroke

Even if you don't actually practise yoga, I believe you can benefit from having some knowledge of how it enables your mind and body to work as a whole. Immediately after my stroke, when I could do very little, I made sure I lifted my weak arm onto a pillow or my table so that I could always see it. This was to remind my brain that it was still attached to me and still part of my body. Even though it was not moving or working normally, it was mine. If you keep reminding your brain, the circuit remains intact, in simple terms. If the eye cannot see it and you can't feel it, it is easy for your brain to just disregard the limb and switch off, just as if it were amputated. I also rubbed my arm with my good hand as often as possible and made my fingers move by lifting them and separating them as they couldn't do anything on their own and I couldn't feel them. Some months later I spilled the contents of a boiling kettle over my hand and watched it blister, yet didn't feel a thing. I would try to look at my foot when I was lifted onto a chair and during visiting time my son would test me by placing his foot and some weight on my foot to see if I could feel anything. I would tell myself that I could, but just before he left he'd inform me that he had been practically treading on my foot for the whole of the visiting session. Obviously I had been none the wiser but all this helped. Perhaps you can understand what I am saying from these personal examples. Without practising yoga prior to my stroke and working with my yoga teacher I wouldn't have known of its importance and benefits.

Suitable Yoga exercises for Stroke Survivors

In most yoga exercises you are encouraged to engage your core muscles, as these are a source of our stability, this is something that as a stroke survivor you should work on to help your stability and improve your mobility.

These core muscles are the ones deep inside your stomach/abdomen and to engage them you pull them in so they feel as if they are touching your spine, this will protect your back.

A basic exercise you can do on your own, is whilst you are sitting in your chair with your hands down by your side, engage your core muscles. Then, taking a deep breath, raise your shoulders as if you are trying to touch your ears with them, hold and then lower whilst breathing out. Repeat building up over time.

A good exercise is sitting on an exercise ball, practise engaging these core muscles. When you have mastered this, holding your stick in both hands rest it on your lap and slowly raise it above your head or as high as you can manage, pause and then lower slowly staying in control. Repeat the exercise a few times to start with, building up over time. When you have mastered this, the next step is, when the stick is above your head, turn from your waist from one side to the other, pausing in the centre with the core muscles still engaged. If you are unable at the start to use your stick, balancing on the ball with your core muscles engaged is an exercise in itself.

Due to muscle weakness, some stroke survivors spend a lot of time sitting with their shoulders often rounded which can cause you to take shallow breaths. To help, with assistance, lie on a firm bed with a rolled up bath towel placed between your shoulder blades going down your back towards your waist, hands down by your sides, take long slow deep breathes as this will open out your rib cage.

A good source for stroke survivors of suitable exercises are available on YouTube.

Meditation

This is a simple practice you can do unaided, or you can be guided by a meditation CD. It helps you to concentrate on an object, sound, your breathing or a visualisation and promotes relaxation and personal and spiritual growth. When you meditate regularly it can reduce neurological disorders and it also helps in the prevention of stroke and gives you a sense of well-being. As we begin to understand more about the mind's role in health and disease it is evident that meditation is very beneficial.

When you meditate, start, if you can, by sitting up with your spine straight, yet relaxed, reducing tension. You can sit in a chair with both feet on the floor if your body allows. I'm still not able to sit cross-legged on the floor. If you are listening to a guided meditation, I suggest you close your eyes, take a few gentle breaths, in and out. I realise this is something we do without thinking but, now, we are going to take a longer breath in through our nose with our mouth closed, hold it for a moment then exhale through your mouth. Repeat this three times releasing any tension with every out-breath (exhalation). If you don't have a guided meditation, you can use music, something that isn't vocal, but which you find soothing and enjoyable. Close your eyes and simply focus on what you are hearing; if your mind begins to wander just acknowledge that and bring back your focus to the music. You can create imagery to match the music and if this happens it can deepen your relaxation. When the music or CD has finished, just sit still for a moment

151

and spend a little time to reflect on how you feel, rather than think, *Oh that's finished* and go on to something else.

You can use a mantra (a short word) in your meditation. Some that I have used in yoga classes are OM, OM AH, SOHAM, OM NAMAH SHIVAYA. It doesn't matter that we don't understand their meaning; they are soft and musical and appear to permeate their sound through our bodies, allowing deeper relaxation and helping to stop our minds from wandering. They are known to give clarity of mind and can clear headaches. It is an approach you will love or hate, but just give it a go. If, for instance, you have chosen OM, you would pronounce it OOOOOOOOM. You'd make it the length of your in breath, then you're out breath and so on, working with what is comfortable for you.

A basic, but very relaxing meditation is Body Asleep, Mind Asleep meditation, something we used to practise at the end of a yoga session. You can practise this either sitting up or lying down. It is good to use at night if you have difficulty sleeping which some stroke survivors have. If you choose to lie down, have your legs slightly apart with your palms facing up as much as you can. I will talk you through the meditation.

Meditation Practice

In order to carry out this meditation you will need to do one of the following as the instructions would be impossible for you to memorise: Either slowly read the instructions into a tape recorder; then play it back and do the exercise. Or use a "buddy system" – you read it to a friend, then he/she reads it to you.

With your eyes closed, take your awareness to your right hand and then slowly in sequence – right thumb, forefinger, middle finger, ring finger, little finger, palm, back of your hand, wrist, forearm, elbow, upper arm, shoulder, right upper back, middle of back, buttock, right thigh, knee, lower leg, ankle, heel, top of foot, big toe, second toe, third toe, fourth toe, little toe and then the whole of the right side of your body. Imagine it all feeling lighter.

Now, in exactly the same way, but slowly moving upwards go through with the left side of your body – both feet and ankles, lower legs, thighs, hips, stomach, small of your back, hands and forearms, shoulders, neck and throat, the back and sides of your head. Stay there for a few moments/breaths then move to your forehead, eyes, ears, nose, cheeks, mouth, and jaw. Then you're whole face and your complete body. Feel the gentle flow of calm breathing and rest. When you feel ready, slowly open your eyes.

Visualisation

This is very powerful as you aid your recovery by simply sitting and doing this. It sends the right messages to your brain.

Visualise yourself recovered, walking and moving, unaided and with ease. See yourself maybe in a garden, smelling the flowers and feeling the touch of the plants as you walk past them. See yourself bending down and picking flowers with your weak hand. Hear the birds singing and feel the fresh air, as you walk, on both sides of your body. You are seeing and feeling yourself complete again and recovered.

See yourself being able to reach out and clutch an object, and bring it towards you, and carry it while you continue walking.

Imagine you being able to drive, fetching the car keys, unlocking the car and climbing into the driver's seat. There is no one else in the car and you are able to drive it to your destination. You hear the engine and radio playing, hear the outside traffic, see the road markings and street signs. Put yourself in the moment.

Do this over and over again and you will be sending and resending positive reinforcing messages to your brain – it is powerful and is proven to work. Injured athletes who cannot train use visualisation to imagine every little bit of their daily training routine, and as a result they lose much less muscle mass and stay fitter than they would if they remained passive and just waited to recover.

Make this part of your daily routine whenever possible. Remember, we spend so much of our time simply sitting on our own. So really, do we have anything to lose by giving visualisation a shot? No, we don't, but I promise we have a lot to gain and sometimes, too, we can simply fall asleep feeling much more positive and have a much needed rest. So, remember to just get into the habit of visualisation; *we are our own healers.* Every time we practise this we are a little step closer to our own goal. Also, think of the hours you spend in hospital waiting rooms, either waiting for your appointment or for transport. What a perfect and positive way to use the time, especially as it is often when you are feeling rather tired. Again, it is one of the few things we can do without asking for others' help.

Emotional Freedom Technique - EFT

If this is something new to you, I ask you to read the whole section before dismissing it as an 'airy fairy' thing!

It works in a similar way to acupuncture but without the use of needles or anything invasive. There are no chemicals so nothing will interfere with your medication. It is also something that a member of your family or a friend can do for you. I will admit that it does sound a bit like 'knit your own yoghurt' but I will tell you that not only has it relieved grown men of their phobias but also war veterans of their Post-Traumatic Stress Disorder and all their associated nightmares, anxiety attacks, depression, and recurring frightening noises; all these have been removed with the help of EFT. These soldiers had been in and out of different therapies over several years and nothing had worked. This alone shows the power and benefits of this technique. In simple terms, the technique involves tapping, humming, counting and saying a few words where necessary.

We have imbalances within our body's energy system which often result in headaches, tiredness or illness. We create a memory pattern within our makeup, our cells. We are the product of our earlier self. So, if we have gone through life struggling with emotions that have hurt or upset us, we act accordingly in our day-to-day decision making, often without realising it. For instance, if we're asked if we'd like to do something or go somewhere, if we're completely carefree we will reply with our inner wish, such as 'Yes, thank you for asking' or 'No, that's not really my cup of tea'. If past experiences have left us feeling a bit downtrodden and with low self-esteem, we may feel an overwhelming desire to please or be worried about upsetting the other person's feelings and agree to something we don't really want to do. I can hear you saying that this is a very simple example but the reality is you haven't been true to yourself; you have acted as you feel you should. When we do this throughout our lives, as we get older we lessen our own value and keep ourselves in the background; and it eventually changes how we appear to others. We find it difficult to accept compliments and are without our own valuable points of view. Then we find we are not treated as we'd hoped to be. More feelings are suppressed and this can overload our bodies and we can become ill. Unless this inbuilt pattern is changed nothing will change. The age-old saying 'Smile and the world will smile with you' is so true. Treat yourself as you want to be treated. Love yourself as you love others. Give yourself the time you give to others and you will see people's behaviour change towards you. It sounds so easy but if it is why are so many of us suffering so many ailments? This is where EFT comes in. It can break that pattern and create your new, happy blueprint.

Your medication from your doctor is working on the chemical nature of your body, and EFT can be working on your energy nature. It can help with fears, phobias, addictions, traumatic memories, physical and emotional healing.

You can go to a practitioner working with alternative treatments like homeopathy, Bowen, Reiki etc. or you can also learn the technique and practise on yourself and your family. It works by tapping on the acupressure points of the body while saying certain words connected to the concerns, phobia or problem. Research shows that as we tap we send a calming message to the fight or flight part of the brain which in simple terms rewires our system.

There is a set-up statement that is used regardless of the situation and that always remains the same as do the pressure points you tap on. It may be advisable to go to a practitioner to begin with, then learn and do it yourself from there.

To find out more about how to practise and gain more knowledge on EFT, simply type EFT into a search engine and you will find there are many books, DVDs and a selection of examples on YouTube. The National Health Service (NHS) in the United Kingdom have started recognising the benefits of EFT in treating depression.

Massage

This is most beneficial for a stroke survivor. I cannot say I find it particularly enjoyable but I know Ron will forgive me here as we do joke that it's nicer to close the door behind him than greet him! For it to be really helpful it needs to be deep tissue massage. For ages you can't feel anything, that's the cruel side of stroke. Then, when you can, it doesn't feel like a gentle massage, it hurts!

I'm not talking about massage for relaxation, rather sports massage. This is the manipulation and stretching of muscles and connective tissue to enhance your movement, something we are struggling with at the moment. This type of massage enables us to get the most out of our muscles, to stretch the muscles we can't stretch by ourselves. When a muscle feels tight, painful or weak it is congested, which means it won't function properly, it could be a result of insufficient use or bad posture. Deep tissue or sports massage as it's more commonly known, releases and aids the lymphatic system, improving circulation.

Acupuncture

This is an ancient Chinese technique which is now used in the National Health Service. What is even better is that you don't really have to believe in it for it to work; just lie back and let it 'do its stuff'. It can be very beneficial for patients who suffer from high tone, for example when you have difficulty in opening the fingers in your hand and keeping your hand open. Low tone (like mine) is when it just flops and hangs limply by your side.

The practitioner uses very thin, stainless steel needles and you rarely feel anything. It might look as if it's going to be unpleasant but it doesn't hurt or leave any marks on your skin. It works by encouraging your body to promote natural healing by inserting the needles at very precise acupressure points.

The Chinese believe that channels of energy run in regular patterns throughout our bodies and when things go wrong blockages are formed which prevent the natural flow of energy. The needles stimulate the nervous system to release chemicals in the spinal cord, muscles and brain, plus releasing hormones and promoting natural healing.

Scenar – Electro-stimulation Therapeutic Medical Device

This is a handheld device, about the size of a remote control, which was invented in Russia to help astronauts deal with the rigours of space travel. The device was developed as part of the Soviet space programme, the goal being to create a highly effective device that could keep the astronauts' health in top form without having to use medicines. It uses biofeedback and stimulates the nervous system, enabling the body to heal itself. It is non-damaging and safe but can't be used if you have a pacemaker. The scenar is brushed over the patient's skin looking for any resistance. Essentially the device is using the patient's own endogenous signals, scanning and retransmitting many times a second. The device "evolves" a new signal pattern for the diseased tissue; it literally enters into an information 'dialogue' with the body and evokes a healing response. It is impossible for the body to resist this, and new frequencies and energy patterns are established. It is said to stimulate neuropeptides in damaged cells. This healing process continues for a time after the treatment has finished too. Depending on the degree of your condition it may take several treatments. It is obviously more complex than this but that is an overview. For me personally, the reality of beneficial improvements I have experienced from this form of treatment/therapy has been amazing. I will never forget the day we witnessed the first flicker of movement in a finger on my right hand. The experience is surreal: watching a part of your hand move and you are not in control of this movement taking place, or the extent of it, or when it will cease. It brought tears of joy to my eyes and strengthened my hope of regaining full movement in my hand.

There are several practitioners in the UK working from private clinics; you can find out if there is one near you by going online. There are a handful in the US where it has 'light touch' Food and Drug Administration (FDA) approval as a relaxant and a 'muscle re-educator'.

Things to remember:

- research the benefits of alternative treatments, don't readily dismiss
- whenever possible use visualisation, e.g., seeing yourself walking unaided, driving again
- think about something relaxing and focus on this solely until it takes the mind away from your worries
- carry out the breathing techniques regularly, especially when stressed

Chapter Fifteen

The Importance of a Healthy Diet

'Let food be thy medicine, and medicine be thy food.'
Hippocrates

Vitamins

It is more important than ever to make sure your diet is providing all the necessary vitamins and minerals as most of us aren't able to take vitamin supplements because of the medication we're on.

There are two types of vitamins. Water soluble: Vitamin C, B complex and Folic Acid. And fat soluble – Vitamins A, D, E and K.

Water soluble vitamins are easily lost by overcooking food or leaving it exposed to air. They need to be eaten daily as the body can't store them. If you overeat these vitamins they are not harmful as the body disposes of the excess when you pass urine.

Fat soluble vitamins are found mainly in fatty foods and can be stored in your liver and called upon when required. If eaten in excess and too many are therefore stored in the liver they can be harmful.

N.B. To absorb vitamin D you need vitamin C at the same time.
(Your recommended daily dose will be detailed on the products you buy.)

Vitamin A

Very important for us as it helps strengthen our immune system. It also aids night vision, skin and the linings of the nose.

Good sources: cheese, liver, oily fish, milk, low-fat spreads, yoghurt.

Vitamin B group and Folic Acid

B1 – Thiamine

Can be found in most foods and so is easily obtained. It needs to be eaten daily as it cannot be stored in the body. It helps to break down and release energy from food but also keeps nerves and muscle tissue healthy, which is very important to us as we are not doing weight bearing exercises and building muscle, or maintaining ourselves easily at the moment.

Good sources: pork, vegetables, milk, cheese (watch the amount because of cholesterol levels), peas, fresh and dried fruit especially apricots, eggs, wholegrain bread, breakfast cereals.

B2 – Riboflavin

Produces the body's own steroids and red blood cells. It also helps to maintain healthy skin, eyes and our nervous system. Sunlight can destroy this vitamin so these foods should not be left in the sunshine.

Good sources: mushrooms, rice, milk, breakfast cereals, eggs.

B3 Niacin

Also helps the nervous system as well as the digestive system and produces energy from the food we eat.

Good sources: meat, fish, eggs, milk.

B6

Helps the body to convert and store energy from carbohydrates and helps form haemoglobin.

Good sources: chicken, pork, cod, turkey, whole cereals, bread, rice, eggs, vegetables, soya beans, peanuts, milk, potatoes.

B12

Helps to keep your nervous system healthy, makes blood cells, releases energy from our food and processes Folic acid which helps prevent anaemia.

Good sources: meat, salmon, cod, milk, cheese, eggs, yeast extract, some breakfast cereals.

Folic Acid

Works alongside Vitamin B12 to help form healthy red blood cells and reduce problems with our nervous system.

Good sources: broccoli, sprouts, asparagus, peas, chickpeas, brown rice, breakfast cereals.

Pantothenic acid

Also releases energy from our food and is found in many meats and vegetables. It cannot be stored and therefore needs to be eaten daily. *Good sources:* chicken, beef, lamb, kidneys, potatoes, porridge, tomatoes, eggs, broccoli, brown bread, rice.

Vitamin C (Ascorbic acid)

Helps us keep all our cells healthy and maintains our connective tissue. You need to eat it daily as it cannot be stored, but don't overeat it as you might get an upset stomach or stomach pain.

Good sources: dark leafy greens – kale, broccoli, Brussels sprouts. kiwi fruit, citrus fruits – oranges, clementines, tangerines, strawberries, hot chilli peppers, bell peppers, guavas, fresh herbs - thyme & parsley

Vitamin D

Helps to regulate the amount of phosphate and calcium in your body. It's very important for us as lack of exercise can reduce the strength in our bones and it is especially crucial right before and after menopause for women. It is absorbed by the skin when we sit in the sunshine, and is why we need exposure to sunlight whenever we can, so long as we have sun lotion on. Don't have too much, though, as it can build up in your kidneys and have the reverse effect.

Good sources: oily fish, eggs, fat spreads, breakfast cereals.

Vitamin E

Helps to protect cells and can be stored in the body.
Good sources: cereals, seeds.

Vitamin K

Particularly important for us as it helps with the clotting of blood and the healing of wounds. It also helps in bone strength. We produce our own Vitamin K from the healthy bacteria in our bowel. It can be stored in the body as well.

Good sources: green leafy vegetables, cereals, vegetable oils, dairy products, meat.

Calcium

Important in helping to regulate our heartbeat, muscle contractions, normal blood clotting and aids healthy bones and teeth. It maintains and lowers blood pressure and even protects us against colon and breast cancer.

Good sources: milk, green leafy vegetables, tofu, soya beans, nuts, fish like sardines, salmon, perch, rainbow trout.

Healthy Snacks

We all like to have snacks between meals but it is so easy to reach for sweet sugary things that taste good and satisfy hunger pangs initially but then cause sugar dips and make us crave even more. If you change your snacking habits, you will not only feel full for longer, but also be helping to maintain your overall health.

Examples:

Nuts, seeds (sources of vitamin E) and **dark chocolate**

Contain antioxidants that can enhance our concentration, which is something we all need help with. An ounce of each of these give us all the benefits without the sugars, fat and calories of other snacks.

Blueberries

Great on your cereal or in a pudding or just as a snack; helps your brain function well, and are also an antioxidant.

Avocados

Very filling and satisfying and help reduce the risk of bad cholesterol.

Almonds

(Note: do not eat the blanched type as they are to be used in cooking and are too difficult for the kidneys to break down.) A tasty, filling snack and packed with benefits. They are good for the brain and regulate cholesterol and blood pressure levels. They also help to prevent cancer and diabetes, help with weight loss, boost energy and prevent constipation.

Dried apricots

Contain vitamins C and K, potassium and iron and are low in calories. They can act as a gentle laxative if you have 6-8 a day, and can help ease digestion. They are also good for people who are prone to anaemia. Apricot juice with honey can help cool your body during a fever.

Sultanas

High in energy and minerals, an antioxidant, and low in fat.

Pumpkin seeds

Full of antioxidants, vitamins A and E, and good for lowering cholesterol and boosting your immune system.

Sesame seeds

Contain calcium.

Linseed

Add to your cereal as they contain omega 3.

Coconut

High in fibre, vitamins and minerals and very nutritious.

Bananas

High in B6 and a filling snack and contain 11% of your daily fibre requirement. They help maintain low blood sugar as they contain a high level of potassium. They help regulate the body's salt level and allow healthy amounts of calcium to stay in the body. They stimulate mucus in the stomach thus protecting it against acids and help increase healthy bacteria.

Oranges

Contain vitamins A, B, C and B complex, small amounts of potassium, iron, phosphorous, calcium and fibre. A regular intake of orange juice helps to prevent kidney disease and kidney stones. The calcium helps your bones and teeth and the iron and B6 helps produce haemoglobin.

Apples

A good source of Vitamins C and D with small amounts of potassium, phosphorous, calcium and fibre. Apples contain something called 'boron' which is believed to strengthen bones; and they also contain quercetin which may protect brain cells from free radical damage which may lead to Alzheimer's. People who eat two apples a day may lower their cholesterol by as much as 16%. The pectin in apples lowers the body's need for insulin and therefore helps in the management of diabetes.

Kiwi fruit

High in vitamins A, C and E and also contain a small amount of serotonin which helps us to feel calmer and happier. If you eat two or three kiwi fruit a day you can improve your heart by thinning blood, reducing clotting and lowering the amount of fat. They also improve the health of your respiratory tract, immune system, improve nerve function, and help people with depression.

Pears

High in fibre and vitamins B complex and C and have some vitamin A. They help boost your immune system and are a good source of boron that helps the body retain calcium which is good in the prevention of osteoporosis. The high fibre helps maintain a healthy digestive system and are good for the prevention of cancer. The vitamin C promotes colon health.

Things to remember:

- next time you reach for a snack think about what you are having
- look for healthy alternatives to daily snacks which aid recovery
- think about the food your body really needs

Chapter Sixteen

Now or Never - Going Solo

'Success is not final, failure is not fatal: it is the courage to continue that counts.'
Winston Churchill

It has been pointed out that I have been very brave and determined in so many areas. Yet, when it comes to going out on my own, I still haven't mastered this one, and it's now close to three years since my last stroke.

Recently, on returning home from my stroke group I thought about Jim, a fellow group member, and how much I admired the way he has been out to the shopping centres on his own. Better still, he has travelled half way across the county, alone, on public transport by both train and bus. Yet here am I admiring his achievements and finding reasons not to attempt them myself. I cannot preach, 'Push yourself' and not carry it out myself. So, I have to bite the bullet and do something about it.

Well, a few sleepless nights built up and I decided to challenge myself. My friend, Jacques, often works abroad and has asked if I would like to join him, but I always politely decline. I know I wouldn't be able to attempt a long car journey but he tells me he's about to leave for Dublin which is only a forty minute flight away with a hotel ten minutes from the airport. He and Nick think this is a brilliant idea and say it would be great if I could find an Irish bar which Nick could visit one day – that would be my task. This would have been easy in days of old but scary beyond belief in today's world. Could I make them understand? No, of course I couldn't. They had decided I was going and that was that.

Well, ten minutes before Jacques was due to pick me up, I hadn't completely finished my packing as I still wasn't sure I was going. Henry was home and had been primed to make sure I got in the car and went on my way. Tammie, my friend, was with us, and she and Henry saw us off. It was real; the journey began.

At the airport we were greeted by the wheelchair assistance service which was second to none. The member of the staff was so friendly, cheerful and patient. Once on the flight there was no backing out despite my nerves kicking in big time. This was it.

However, before we'd even finished our drink and chocolate bars it was time to land. We had to wait a while for the wheelchair assistance service to help me disembark, and I saw this as my chance to quickly get the return flight home – I'd touched down on Irish soil and been to Dublin! But Jacques was busy organising a taxi so we were soon on our way to the hotel.

The hotel turned out to be full of activity, noise and jollity as the Irish Paralympic Team was having a huge send-off party, so the place was full of disabled people. Suddenly, I was not the only one who stood out, rather Jacques, who was able-bodied.

We had our meal and suddenly I felt exhausted and had to go to sleep. The following morning I awoke thinking it must have been about nine but soon saw it was nearly eleven. I couldn't believe how late it was. I needed to get up and dressed and get something to eat. Jacques had already been at work for three hours. I had to see and learn about Dublin and also find Nick's Irish bar before meeting up with Jacques, and by the time I would be dressed it would be nearly lunchtime.

Finally ready, I ventured out and made my way to the lifts. My heart sank as I realised how big the hotel was. If I felt this here, how huge and daunting would the centre of Dublin be? I thought about going back to my room, googling 'Dublin', learning all I needed to know, and I'd be completely safe and no one would be any the wiser. But, I needed food and I'd missed breakfast. I took the lift down and plucked up the courage to talk to the receptionist. I told her my fears about not being able to get on a bus, remembering things and so on. We wrote down the name of the hotel with my room number and she phoned for a taxi. By the time I turned round it was there.

The cab driver was wonderful. He took me to the city centre and to the tour bus. They lowered the step to the bus to enable me to get on and he also helped me. Not only that, he also spoke to the bus driver explaining how I needed help, creating a sort of safety-blanket for me. We decided that I would tap my stick in a certain way when I wished to get off. While helping me, he'd left his cab immediately next to the bus with its door wide open. He kept saying, 'Don't worry, let's just make sure you are safe and can get on'. Such kindness.

I was now on a bus travelling around Dublin. The tour bus lets you hop on and off wherever you like and visit certain places, and operates until 5.30. I did consider staying on for the rest of the day as I felt self-conscious about tapping the stick. I went on one trip around the city and was then so tired from the build-up and the journey that I could have used a nap. Then I felt the need for both food and the toilet and was forced to ask for help to get off.

From there, I could see Grafton Street across the road. But that was the problem; I was on the wrong side. Just then, I saw two policemen and asked if they were crossing over and would they take me, too? At first, they looked a little surprised at my request but helped all the same. Safely over, I looked up the famous street which seemed much quieter than any other in Dublin but there were still lots of people. To my right was a department store, Brown Thomas, which looked quiet and calm in comparison so I decided that would be my safe haven as there was bound to be a coffee shop inside. I made it easily and it was all on level ground with no steps to battle with and I quickly found a seat. There was also waitress service. I stayed there and felt very tired by this stage. I couldn't go into other shops or bars as they were too busy with self-service bars on different levels where you had to stand. I had gone out on my own but these were impossible for me to handle.

I still had my task of finding Nick's bar and also a place to eat that evening but, to be honest, all I actually wanted to do was sleep; I was exhausted. When the waitress brought my food I asked her both questions and was overheard by a very kind lady at the next table. Later on, before she left, she came and sat next to me and told me not to go into O'Connell Street on my own, as it was not safe and somewhere I shouldn't be. I promised I wouldn't. She suggested a nearby restaurant and the Westbury Hotel where I could sit and wait for my friend. She needn't have worried as I wasn't going anywhere.

After she left, a man about my age came over and said, 'That lady knows what she's talking about, please listen'. I wished I had asked the lady's name but I thank her now; I took her advice. To add to the day my phone battery was nearly flat but I managed to inform Jacques of the change of plan and the meeting place. Luckily, he came and found me since he was not able to call me.

We went into Bewleys on Grafton Street for supper. It was lively and atmospheric with high ceilings and huge, stained-glass windows and served Italian food. The only Irish thing on the menu was Guinness. Jacques insisted I try Guinness – I couldn't be in Dublin and not have one, so this was the time. He even took a photo of me drinking it for proof.

During the meal, we chatted about each other's day and then about my stroke and how far I had come since those early days when Jacques had pushed me around in the wheelchair. He also told me about something I hadn't known before. He said that at first he just couldn't believe that I'd had a stroke. He couldn't accept that it was me, his fit, healthy and sporty friend. Sorry, they had to have made a mistake; it was someone else. It didn't dawn on me that it would be such a shock, a bolt out of the blue, to my friends, too. I don't know why I hadn't thought about my friends' feeling this way. I

173

suppose I just didn't appreciate that it had an impact on their lives, if that makes sense.

It was quite early when we finished our meal and then fatigue took a hold over me. I could not battle it any longer and seriously needed to sleep. I couldn't stay awake a minute longer and needed to be in a taxi immediately and just lying down. It had been an exhausting day - yet one of huge achievement. Right then I was too tired to realise that. Once back, I struggled to get ready for bed and longed to get into it. I then fell asleep as soon as my head hit the pillow.

The following morning we had to be at the airport early and I had been concerned about this as my brain doesn't function well first thing in the morning, and I feel unwell if I push myself. I did manage to be up and ready on time but I feel, as I write this, that I must apologise to Jacques, who was accompanying me home, as I may have been a little short in the car. He had asked if we could stop for breakfast on the way home and I just replied 'no'. I wouldn't normally be so selfish but I just felt I had to be home and in bed; not only was I feeling sick but I had a pain in my head. I didn't tell him because I was trying to fight it and by discussing it I would acknowledge it.

Once we reached home, Nick made drinks and prepared a little breakfast for Jacques. I was in bed very soon and slept for most of the day. When I woke that evening and spoke to Nick about the trip I began to feel a sense of achievement but I was still very tired. Nick was extremely pleased and suggested we return one day and go into the bar that he'd asked me to find. I remained tired for three days and slept all of the first day, but I can now say that I have ventured out alone and conquered my fear. I will admit, though, to still feeling nervous and vulnerable and although I did it all in one huge FIRST, I chose one of the safest and kindest places to go.

Things to remember:

- don't put off things that make you nervous
- conquer your fears
- the longer you put things off the greater the fear will become
- fighting the fear and biting the bullet is exhausting but rewarding

Chapter Seventeen

Sources of Support and Help

'Wherever we look upon this earth, the opportunities take shape within the problems.'
Nelson A. Rockefeller

Brain Group

I am fortunate to have been able to go to this group as it has huge benefits. It represents another journey as all of us who go there are affected differently by our strokes. We have different tasks to work on within our own programmes but they do sometimes overlap. It can be an emotional jolt to learn that you have yet more difficulties to overcome that you weren't even aware of. But, without having had the opportunity of attending the group I wouldn't have had the chance of facing and correcting those difficulties.

Within the group we also have the time to talk amongst ourselves about our situations and challenges and how we have dealt with them, and the emotions which we have experienced or missed. At one meeting a fellow member and I discussed how our roles as parents had changed and how we no longer felt of any real use or benefit. We felt that our sons and daughters may be thinking, 'it isn't worth asking them because they can't drive / can't answer like they used to...' Now, that may not be how our children see us but that is how we now feel. Thanks to the group we were able to have that discussion which wouldn't have come up in any other kind of conversation where people just wouldn't be able to really understand.

We all suffer from what is called an ABI – an acquired brain injury. This is an injury to the brain that is not either hereditary, degenerative, congenital or caused by trauma at birth; it is caused afterwards by our stroke.

Stroke Club

These should be available locally, but you can check your nearest club via the Internet or with the Stroke Association, where you can also request a quarterly Stroke Magazine. .

Stroke Association Awards

This group usually meets every week or two weeks depending on where you live. It again gives you the opportunity to get out and meet other similar people, and the lovely thing is that they are of all ages and who may have had their stroke 10 or more years ago, so you can learn of so many beneficial ways towards recovery.

The Stroke Association in the UK runs an annual awards ceremony which has many different categories, it is a charity supporting Stroke survivors, families & carers. It promotes life after stroke. Candidates can be nominated by family, friends, or in my case a member of the association nominated me in the "Courage Award" category. The major ceremony for "stroke Person of the Year" is held in London but there are also regional ceremonies where awards for the category of which I was a nominee are given. We were doubly fortunate as at the same event my Stroke Group also received an award.

Different Strokes

Is a registered charity established in 1996 by a small group of younger stroke survivors which provides a unique, free service throughout the United Kingdom for those in a similar situation. They offer information packs, access to exercise and support groups along with a counselling service.

Local Colleges

Most have courses for the disabled, and you can ask about these at your Stroke Club. They have photography, cookery, woodwork courses regularly. There are also Lunch Clubs that are organised weekly again through the Stroke Club; all very beneficial for practicing speech and confidence in going out as well as just seeing people regularly.

Hydrotherapy

Find out where you're nearest hydro pool is - not all hospitals have them. You may find that they have pay drop in sessions a couple or one night a week so that you can practise your exercises given by your physiotherapist, or just go along for confidence building.

Headway

Once other sources of assistance ceased, Headway was in place to help. This is an organisation which is available to people with any type of brain injury. They have clay sessions, painting, social gatherings, discussion groups, and other facilities depending on each group. They also have counsellors to talk to - both stroke survivors and their family members. This is particularly useful for the carer. The stroke survivor, remember, has physios and others to talk to most of the time, unlike the carer who is on their own from day one.

They run all-day classes in many locations, so your carer can find out what is available that might be of interest to you. You do not have to go for a full day, you can just attend morning or afternoon. I know they have pottery classes because I have attended those, they are an enjoyable way to be doing physiotherapy on the hand without it feeling like physio; then you all have coffee and biscuits. They also have history and gardening groups among others available. You have one or two carers assigned to come to you in your home, and they will help you with things within the home, take you shopping, etc.

Neuro-Physiotherapy

You may also start outpatient neuro-physio at this stage. There is a waiting list for this so ask your physiotherapist to put you on the list before you actually need it so hopefully the timing will be right. There is hospital transport available to stroke survivors; again your physiotherapist will have a leaflet for you from your local hospital, or the one you book them from. Your stroke support worker may also have this information.

What can you do to help yourself along with all of this? Make sure you do all your exercises daily that you're physiotherapist has written for you. Some days you won't feel like it, I know only too well, but it does pay off.

Things to remember:

- attend groups with fellow survivors
- find colleges that hold courses for the disabled
- do exercises regularly at home

Chapter Eighteen

Friends' Views

'Man's friendships are one of the best measures of his worth'
Charles Darwin

Sabine

Across the field there is someone on a horse. I cannot see who it is as the

Pre-Stroke

trot speeds to a gallop. It is wonderful to watch a fast powerful horse, its flying hooves lifting earth high into the sky. Both horse and rider work in harmony yet there is total control of the animal. The horse's muscles glisten with perspiration, exerting all their strength to the upmost. The rider applies laser like concentration, living in that very moment as nothing else matters. This is an abiding

memory of Sas before her life was to change.

I hear that Sas is not well and has been taken to the hospital. When first told that she has suffered a stroke, I am numb. Sheer disbelief follows: no one so energetic can have a stroke. They only happen to the elderly, not to the fit, healthy and young. My tears follow.

There is some small relief. Although the stroke is serious, Sas is conscious. When I am allowed to visit her in hospital, I fight to put on a brave face but still my eyes swell with tears. Yesterday I saw an attractive woman leading an active, busy lifestyle. Now I see my friend who can hardly move and is dependent on others to get up. Her speech is slow and confusing; her mouth lopsided and her right eye glazed. It seems to look right through me. She cannot feel let alone move the right hand side of her body. Her hearing has been affected. Above all she is in pain, so excruciating that the only relief comes from morphine. And yet her first concern is how I am and how my day has been.

When finally discharged from the hospital the days, weeks and months ahead are slow. Nurses come twice a day to help with basic care. Occupational and physiotherapists attend to try to rebuild that which has been so suddenly lost.

I cannot conceive what it must be like to have your world turned upside down. In a matter of seconds to become practically, and financially dependent on others, and yet, despite all that has happened, there prevails a feeling of strength. Could it be the stiff British upper lip? Is it pretence to knuckle down and get on with things, but all the time crying inside?

I ask myself this question all the time. I certainly know how I would feel: constant questioning of my fate through tears of rage. Why did it happen to me?

Sas had a strict upbringing. There was no time for any 'nonsense'. No malingering and no self-pity. Yet she was not emotionally starved, nor is she unable to show her emotions. Quite the opposite, her empathy for others only makes her acutely aware of her own feelings, but I do not see any tears. Is she going through some sort of cycle similar to those who suffer a bereavement? Will she eventually have a breakdown? I do worry so about this but only time will tell.

Time goes by. Despite making incredible physical progress, there is a period when I feel Sas has reached a plateau. I am relieved to some extent that the emotions have caught up with her but I worry that she is spiralling downwards towards depression. I had thought that this was inevitable after all she had gone through, but perhaps bizarrely, also as something positive. There really HAD to be a safety valve. Stiff upper lip, positive outlook or not, the emotional tension simply had to be released.

And I am glad she did! However hard, emotions should never be suppressed or defeated. Like a river heading to the sea, they have to find an outlet to escape. It is one of life's few truths that it is always better when we have finally succumbed to them. Only then can we break free and start anew.

It is now a few years ago since Sas's first stroke. Her 'post-stroke life' has been in so many ways a voyage of discovery: to see what and indeed who matters in life, how to overcome obstacles, to be amazed by our bodies and brain and to give them the respect they deserve.

If it had not been for her stroke would she have ever realised that she has hidden talents, such as painting? Or indeed such inner strength and optimism to be positive even at the bleakest moments? Would she have ever written a book to help others?

None of us know what might happen to us: illness may strike anyone at any time. However, if it does, we can always choose not to be defeated by it.

And I know Sas will never be!

Louise

I first met Sas through mutual friends of ours at their Christmas Drinks Party many years ago. I walked into their sitting room and saw this tall, thin, beautiful girl with an amazing smile and a lovely hairstyle.

We later got talking; I asked Sas what she did and she told me modelling; I remember thinking 'And with a great personality'. Which was no surprise. Sas was very chatty and kind; I asked her what "lotions and potions" she used hoping then I can use the same. She said that good old vitamin E cream is excellent and skin specialists and dermatologists would say the same. I later went out and purchased about four jars!

A few years later our boys attended the same school so I did get to see Sas at the school gates, but not that often. Whenever we did we loved talking about fashion, creams, makeup hair, etc. the boys looking bored in the car. Sas obviously had a successful modelling and television career and leading what must have been a fantastic life to someone like myself at home looking after family, and doing the housekeeping. I always loved to hear about what Sas was doing, where she was. I was always so excited whenever I saw her on QVC, thinking 'That's my friend'. I always call her my 'Model Friend'.

It was of no surprise to me that I went a few months without seeing or passing Sas in her silver soft top sports car, I knew she was busy and so often away. BUT what a shock when I saw Nick at a cricket match our boys were playing in and I asked, 'How's Sas? What glamorous work is she doing now? What programme has she been on recently?' He told me the terrible news that she'd had a stroke. I just could not believe it. This will sound awful but Sas just did not look like someone who would have a stroke in my eyes - beautiful, young, fit, slim, lovely hair. I still think she has lovely hair but it is an ongoing disagreement joke between us. That is so wrong of me though, to think – anyone of us, young, old, fat, thin could have a stroke, you do not have to be a type, it is just that it came as such a shock.

I am a volunteer at our local Stroke Group and have been for some years now. My mom was one of the original volunteers when the group began many years ago. Sas comes to our group and sits at my table; we don't just chat; we do work; honestly Janet. (Janet heads the group.) Sas is not only a great help to me, but to everyone in the group in so many ways. She is always happy to talk to anyone, especially encouraging when new members come for the first few times.
Sas has helped raise money by hosting a fantastic 'tea party' in her home and garden she was blessed with a beautiful sunny day. However, little did we all know that she had been feeling poorly and just returned from seeing the doctor who had suggested she went to the hospital. But again, this is

185

Sas thinking about others and the 'show must go on'. Sas was unwell for weeks following the tea party.

Sas has turned her artwork into Birthday and Christmas greeting cards, again raising money for our group.

Sas has had strokes but to me she is still that chatty and kind person I first met all those years ago. Yes she now walks with the help of wires and a stick, but to be honest I don't see these until she starts moaning about wires showing through tights. We do laugh about things; how she hides the FES device in her bra, the intention to look more normal, but also giving the impression of a bigger bust! Sas just seems to get on with everything. Her determination to do - to get done and complete is a credit to her and her alone.

Sas has a glowing personality; always thinking of others first and just wanting to help.

You are an inspiration to me and I know too many other people 'young and old'

I'm still proud to say you are my 'Model Friend' Sas!

All my love, Louise

Chapter Nineteen

Conclusion - The New Beginning

'There is no failure except in no longer trying.'
Egbert Hubbard

I was in my mid-forties, a working mother previously divorced, living with my son and partner and our dog in Worcestershire. Lovely fresh countryside that we enjoyed walking in when possible, admittedly usually to the local pub, but this was an hour's walk over fields and the same home afterwards, so I always felt we deserved our drink on arrival. I would not have considered myself a prime candidate for stroke as I was very active. I walked regularly, swam and rode a few times a week and practised yoga and Pilates once or twice a week. I have always had a slim build and never smoked. I enjoy my chocolate and cakes but equally love vegetables and fruit too. I enjoy grilled rather than fried foods so in the main my diet was fairly healthy.

When I look back maybe if I hadn't practised yoga I may have been unwell sooner, who knows? Sometimes I'd be racing against traffic to try and make my class, many of which I missed; everyone looking so serene on my arrival, I would be like a whirlwind and late. My heart pounding and my breathing racing but I felt the benefits and so much better by the end of the session. I always slept so much better on those nights.

Pre-stroke I lived life a little like a headless chicken, partly I feel because I was self-employed/freelance. I said yes to all work that came my way not knowing when it wouldn't any longer do so. I had every intention of seeing friends and family, yet didn't achieve it. I was always either travelling on a motorway, racing against some time deadline or staying away. I lived in a home I loved yet spent so little time in it, usually leaving and returning in hours of darkness. I longed to watch my son Henry's rugby and cricket matches yet missed them all. I always remember my sadness when he won the school sports cup and I couldn't be there with other parents to see him being presented with it. Later when he and his friend Jack became Vice Chairman of School, thanks to my post-stroke life, I was there with my friend Kay; two proud mothers together watching and listening as Henry and Jack were presented with the honour; my heart swollen with pride and tears welling that at last I was present to witness one of his achievements.

One year, when on our family holiday in Thailand, we sat in a restaurant which had lovely little messages on the back of its menus. We loved this place and returned several times. Strangely my message more than once was 'Stop and smell the flowers'. There was a message there. Strange too that with three of us sharing a table it was always me who had been given that message. Also the funny thing is I cannot remember any of the other messages we read from those menus.

Also pre-stroke days I had to be so organised; everything had to be done to the best of my ability and finished yesterday! If anyone asked me to do anything I did it even if it was really putting too much pressure on me. I always put everyone else first, ignoring any signals my body may be trying to shout out at me.

I had not realised how life was simply passing me by. I stupidly got caught up in the amount of work I had booked and how organised I was or wasn't; living life to deadlines and lists! The nature of my work was deadlines and perfection; I had not realised that I was expecting it of myself all the time. I did not ever expect it of others yet I put this continual pressure on myself.

I feel my stroke was a huge wake-up call and a second chance to take a good hard look at myself and where I was going wrong before it was too late. Simply, I'm blessed to be given such an opportunity even if there is a difficult and emotional battle that goes hand in hand with it. I am fortunate to have come out the other side; I hope to be a better and nicer person to myself as well as to others, but I am not the one to judge that and as yet I have not been brave enough to actually ask the question! I realise that I worried about what people think; their expectations of me, only now I see that this is such a debilitating way to live. Reflecting on recovery, I realised it is time to cut myself some slack; be kinder, less judgmental, treat myself as I do others.

If reading and learning from my life lesson helps others to listen to their inner voice and change things before illness steps in, then some good has come out of me recounting my journey to recovery. But I hope too that in being able to relate to some of my emotions and battles along the way it will give some encouragement and comfort on those days we feel alone, a little low and wane in our strength to fight on. Keep believing you can do it and you will. I did and I am just an ordinary middle-aged woman with nothing special other than that self-belief. Something that in my pre-stroke days I probably never owned. Another gift of stroke – My stroke of luck!

Acknowledgements

My first acknowledgement and thank you must go to my partner, Nick, whose words were 'I don't do illness,' until he was thrown into the deep end. The support he has shown me has proved him wrong.

Thank you also to my son, Henry, who was approaching his G.C.S.E.s at the time of my stroke. He also had a life challenge of his own to deal with as he was assaulted when out for a meal with friends. This is a lot for a sixteen year old to cope with without suddenly having to take on a caring role for his mother; the person who had been there for him for the past fifteen years now needed his help every day.

A huge thank you to my closest friends who have supported me along the way and given me a talking to when I have needed it and laughed and cried with me along the way. To my brother, Tom, for making me hold on to my self-belief when a certain official maintained I would always be disabled. To my parents for sitting with me and helping in the early days coming home from the hospital. My father recognised little things that made a big difference; these things he had learnt from his own experience of also having had a stroke years earlier.

Thank you to the Intermediate Care Team (ICT) for pushing me as hard as they could and to Jane for being there at the right time when I had my second stroke. To the ambulance and nursing staff, specialists Dr. Phil and Dr. McClung who stuck with me for so long and never gave up on my recovery progress; Dr McClung has listened to my waffling along the way as I struggled for the right words and lost my train of thought.

To Kat, the physiotherapist, who worked at the hydro, who finally resolved the trouble with my hip.

To Marianne, who wrote personal exercises and still asks about me and visits in her own time.

Thank you to Selly Oak hospital and the Functional Electrical Stimulation (FES) equipment that has helped me. Without the transport service of ambulance drivers and volunteers I would not have been able to attend so many appointments.

Thank you to Pat from the Brain Group whom I'm aware I exhausted at times and to the volunteers who make my local stroke group possible.

Thank you to my friends who, after two years, still visit me and take me out; it means so much.

To Louise for her kind words within this book.

To Steve for his alternative treatments. To Eamonn, for the conversation we had only a short time before my second stroke, you know all! To my YPS for the bonfire laughter.

Everyone has helped me so much and I thank you all. If there is anyone I haven't mentioned I apologise; it is not that your input has not been appreciated but simply that my brain still does not recall all it should when I wish.

My thanks, also, to my friend, Sue, without whose patience, input and proofreading this book would not have reached you.

To Jackie and Jan, a couple of old friends who still take me out regularly three years on. Without this I would be isolated and struggling now, thank you both.

To Sabine for ongoing support.

To Doctor Malcolm Jones and Doctor Juliet Evans who checked my references made to any medical terms.

The Stroke Association for recognising my efforts & achievements and for believing in my book.

To Different Strokes for their support in promoting my book.

To my editor Cliff for going that extra mile and more. For his help, advice and support. For treating me like a friend.

About The Author

Sas Freeman previously worked as a photographic model and on television. She also appeared in films and as a double for Emma Thompson in *Brideshead Revisited*. Alongside, she managed teams for companies delivering advertising material for national organisations, client facing where necessary, pitching campaigns.

Sas is an artist who sells her oil paintings which hang in private homes in various parts of the world. Her work is on display in several galleries in the UK. She has donated several pictures to raise money for charity, including one for cancer which now hangs in a home in Barbados, and one to a Hospice which was displayed at a town festival. The image was chosen to be part of a poster to advertise the event. She's had her watercolours turned into cards and sells them in aid of a local stroke group, to help fellow survivors.

She is part of a Regional Health Focus Group, created to raise awareness and funding for the Functional Electronic Stimulator and Selly Oak Hospital Rehabilitation Centre, which treats people across the UK.

In 2013, she was given the Courage Award from the Stroke Association for her valiant efforts shown throughout her recovery. Part of Sas's story was published in the *Worcester Evening News*; and *Different Strokes*, a charity for young stroke survivors who have agreed to promote her book and share her story.

In order to help fellow survivors at the beginning of their recovery, when they are often unable to read, she is looking to find funding to turn her book, *Two Strokes Not Out*, into an audio version.

To help those who have suffered a stroke and to raise awareness of what can be achieved, she will be working with organisations giving talks to inspire, encourage, and help fellow survivors.

Useful Information

United Kingdom

Action for Dysphasic Adults 1 Royal Street, London SE1 7LL. 0207 261 9572

Assist UK -1 Portland Street, Manchester, M1 3BE

British Aphasia Society, Department of Clinical Communication Studies, City University, Northampton Square. London EC1V 0HB. 0207 477 8000

British Association for Counselling and Psychotherapy BACP House, 35-37 Albert Street, Ruby, Warwickshire CV21 2SG Tel 0870 443 5252

British Association for Counselling 1 Regent Place, Rugby, Warwickshire CV21 2PJ. 01788 578328

British Neuroscience Association Sherrington Buildings, Ashton Street, Liverpool L69 3GE

Care Association of Independent Care Advisors, Orchard House, Albury, Surrey GU5 9AG

Careers National Association 20-25 Glasshouse Yard London EC1 4JS. 0207 4908818

Carers UK, 20-25 Glasshouse Yard, London EC1A 4 JT Tel 020 7490 8818

Chartered Society of Physiotherapy 14 Bedford Row London WC1R 4ED. 0207 306 6666

Chest Heart & Stroke Scotland, 65 North Castle Street Edinburgh, EH2 3LT. 0131 225 6963

Clinical hypnotherapy BST Foundation, 5 Kingsholm House, 106 Ridgeway, Wimbledon London SW1 4RD Tel 020 8946 1432

College of Occupational Therapists 6-8 Marshalsea Road. London SE1 1HL 0207 3576480

Connect 16-18 Marshalsea Road, Southark London SE1 1HL Tel 020 7367 0840

Continence Foundation 2 Doughty Street, London WC 1N 2PH. 0207 404 6875

Crossroads Association of Care Attendants Schemes Ltd 10 Regent Place Rugby, Warwickshire CV21 2PN 01788 573 653

Department of Health, Richmond House, 79 Whitehall, London SW1A 2NL Tel 020 7210 4850

Department of Social Security Disability Unit, The Adelphi 1-11 John Adam Street London WC2N 6HT 0207 712 062

Dial UK – St Catherine's Tickhill Road, Doncaster DN4 8QN

Different Strokes Sir Walter Scott House, 2 Broadway Market, London E8 4QJ. 0207 249 6645

Different Strokes Central Services, 9 cannon Harnett Court, Wolverton Mill, Milton Keynes MK12 5NF Tel: 0845 130 7172 or 01908 317618 www.differentstrokes.co.uk

Disability Alliance First Floor, Universal House, 88-94 Wentworth Street. London E1 7SA

Disabled Drivers Association Ashwellthorpe Norwich. NR16 1EX 01508 489449

Disabled Living Foundation 389-384 Harrow Road, London W9 2HU Tel 0207289 6111

DLF 40 - A charity providing advice on mobility & disability aids & equipment. Disabled Living foundation, 380-384 Harrow Road, W9 2HU

DM UK - The charity for disabled, drivers, passengers and blue badge holders. Disabled motoring UK, Ashwellthorpe, Norwich, NR16 1EX

Employment Opportunities, 53 New Broad Street, London EC2 1SL. Tel 020 7448 5420

Gardening for the disabled www.gardeningfordisabledtrust.org.uk

Keep Able, Flemming Close, park Close Park Farm, Wellingborough Northampton NN8 3BR. 01933 679 426

Mavis-Mobility Advice Vehicle information Service Crowthorne Berkshire RG45 6AU. 01344 770456

Mobility Information Service, National Mobility Centre, Unit 2a, Atcham Estate, Shrewsbury SY4 4UG. 01743 761 889

Motability - Motability Operations, City Gate House, 22 Southwark Bridge Road, London, SE1 9HB

Motability 2nd Floor Gate House, Harlow Essex CM20 1HR

National Council for Voluntary Organisations Regents Wharf 8 All Saints Street London N1 9 RL Tel 0800 2 798 798 (Freephone)

PALS – C/O Staffordshire Moorlands Community & Voluntary Service, Bank House, 20 St Edmund Street, Leek, Staffordshire. ST13 5DS

RADAR Royal Association for Disability and Rehabilitation 12 City Forum, 250 City Road, London EC1V 8AF. 0207 250 3222

Registered Nursing Homes Association, 15 Highfield Road, Edgbaston, Birmingham B15 3 DU Tel 0121 454 2511

Rehab UK Windermere House, Kendel Avenue, London W3 0XA 020 8896 2444

REMAP – providing equipment helping people with disabilities. D9 Chaucer Business Park, Kemsing, Sevenoaks, TN15 6YU

Royal College of Speech & Language therapists, 7 Bath Place, Rivington Street, London EC2A 3DR 0207 613 3855

The Disability Information Trust Mary Marlborough Centre, Nuffield Orthopaedic Centre, Headington Oxford OX3 7LD.

The Patients Association – PO Box 935, Harrow Middlesex, HA1 3YJ

The Stroke Association – 240 City Road, London. EC1V 2PR Tel: 0303 3033100 www.stroke.org.uk

Thrive to Change Lives The Geofrey Udall Centre, Beechill, Reading. RG7 2AT www.thrive.org.uk

United Kingdom Homecare Association 42b Banstead Road, Carshalton Beeches, Surrey SM5 3NW Tel 020 8288 1551

Ireland

Irish Heart Foundation, 4 Clyde Road, Ballsbridge Dublin 4 Tel 01 668 5001

Headway 1-3 Manor Business Park, Manor Street, Dublin 7 Tel 01 810 2066

USA

American Council for Headache Education 19 Mantua Road, Mt. Royal, NI 08061 Tel 856 423 0258

American Health Assistance Foundation, 22512 Gateway Centre Drive Clarksburg, MD 20871 Tel 301 948 3244

American Occupational Therapy Association 4720 Montgomery Lane PO Box 31220 Bethesda, MD 20824-1220 Tel 301 652 2682

American Physiotherapy Association 1111 North Fairfax Street Alexandria, VA 22314-1488 Tel 800 999 2782

American Speech- language - hearing Association 10801 Rockville Pike Rockville, MD 20852 Tel 800 638 8255 (Toll Free)

American Stroke Association 7272 Greenville Avenue, Dallas, TX 75231 Tel 800 242 1871

Association for Driver Rehabilitation Specialists 711 S Vienna Street Rushton, LA 71279 Tel 800 290 2344 (Toll Free)

Brain Aneurysm Foundation, 12 Clarendon Street, Boston, MA 0211 Tel 617 723 3870

Hazel K Goddess Fund for Stroke Research for Women, 785 Park Avenue New York NY 10021-3552 Tel 212 734 8067

Heart Support of America, 6344 Clinton Highway Knoxville, TN 37912 Tel 865 938 5838

KZN Heart Foundation PO Box 3120, Durban 40000 Entabeni Hospital, Central Medical Suite Room 202 2nd Floor 148 Bridge Road Durban 4001 Tel031 261 9055

National Aphasia Association PO Box 1887, Murray Hill Station, New York, NY 10156 Tel 800 922 4622 (Toll Free)

National Council on Aging, 300 D Street SW, Suite 801 Washington, DC20924 Tel 202 479 1200

National Family Caregivers Association 10400 Connecticut Avenue, Suite 500 Kensington, MD 20895 (Toll Free)

National Heart Lung and Blood Institute, PO Box 30105, Bethesda, MD 20824-0105 Tel 301 592 8573

National Institute of Neurological Disorders and Stroke Neurological Institute, PO Box 5801 Bethesda, MD 20824 Tel 301 496 5751

National Rehabilitation Information Centre 4200 Forbes Boulevard, Suite 202 Langham, MD 29706-4829 Tel 301 459 5900

National Stroke Association 9707 East Easter Lane, Englewood, Co 80112 Tel 800 787 6537 (Toll Free)

The Well Spouse Foundation 63 West Main Street, Suite H Freehold, NJ 07728 Tel 800 838 0879 (Toll free)

US Department of Labour Frances Perkins Building, 200 Constitution Avenue, NW Washington, DC 20210 Tel 866 633 7365 (Toll Free)

South Africa

The Stroke Association South Africa, Unit 411, Old Castle Brewery, 6 Beach Road, Woodstock, Cape Town 7924 Tel 021 447 6268

New Zealand

The Stroke Foundation, Midland Region Inc PO Box 990 Tauranga Tel 07 571 3061

Australia

Acquired Brain Injury Service, Arbias, PO Box 213 Fitzroy, VIC 3065 Tel 03 9417 7071

Anxiety Treatment Australia, Floor 1, 140-142 Barkers Road Hawthorn, VIC 3122 Tel 03 9819 3671

Australian Physiotherapy Association Level 3, 201 Fitzroy Street, St Kildare Melbourne, VIC 182 Tel 03 9534 9400

Carers Australia PO Box 73, Deakin West, ACT 2690 Tel 02 6122 9900

Heart Support Australia PO Box 266, Mawson, ACT 2607 Tel 02 6285 2357

Lifeline Australia National Office PO Box 173, Deakin, ACT 2699 Tel 02 6215 9400

National Stroke Foundation Level 3 167-169 Queen Street Melbourne, VIC 3000 Tel 03 9670 10000

Physical Disability Council of Australia PO Box 77 Northgate, QLD 4013 Tel 07 32671057

Speech Pathology Australia 2nd Floor, 11-19 Bank Place Melbourne, VIC 3000 Tel 03 9642 4899

Canada

Heart and Stroke Foundation of Canada, 222 Queen Street, Suite 1402 Ottawa, ON KIP 5V9 Tel 613 569 4361

Neurological Rehabilitation Institute of Ontario, 59 Beaver Bend Crescent, Etobicoke, ON M9B 5R2 Tel 1800 561 9158

Glossary of Terms

Words that doctors and other medical staff may use when explaining things to you and your family.

Agraphia – an acquired inability to write

Alexia – an acquired inability to read

Amnesia - failure of part of memory system

Aneurysm - the ballooning out of the wall of an artery

Angiogram - an X-ray of the artery

Anosmia – absence of the sense of smell

Apraxia – an inability to make skilled movements with accuracy

Ataxia - lack of coordination

Anomia - difficulty finding the correct word

Aphasia - inability to speak

Atrial fibrillation - occurs when the electrical signals in the heart become disorganised, overriding the heart's normal rate and rhythm. This causes the heart to beat irregularly, known as fibrillation.

Bilateral - both sides of the body

Brainstem - lower part of the brain just above the spinal cord

Capillary - tiny blood vessel

Cardiovascular - relating to the heart and blood vessels

Carotid artery - one of two arteries running up the side of the neck carrying blood to the brain

Catheter - small tube inserted into the bladder to drain urine

Cerebellum - located at the bottom back of the brain, it controls movement

Cerebral cortex - outer layer of the upper part of the brain

Cerebral haemorrhage - a bleeding into the brain

Cerebral hemisphere - one of the two halves of the brain (these are joined by nerve fibres)

Cerebral infarct - the area of the brain where the cells have died off

Cerebral oedema - swelling of the brain

Cerebral thrombosis - clotting of an artery

CVA - term often now used for stroke

Cerebrum - the upper part of the brain

Cholesterol - fat found inside the body

Circulatory system - the body's mechanism for circulating blood

Cognitive function - awareness, memory, problem solving, learning, reasoning

Colour agnosia - difficulty remembering or recognising colours

Coma - state of unconsciousness

Contraction of muscle - shortening of fibres, tightness, pulling

Coordination - brain process enabling the body to move and function smoothly and with ease

CT (computerised tomography) - brain X-ray identifying changes within the brain

Disability - a difficulty or defect in normal function of the brain, body or both

Disinhibition - lack of self-control

Dysarthria - weakness in the tongue, jaw or voice box making speech difficult

Drop foot - a foot that falls limp when the leg is lifted

Dyslipidaemia - abnormality in blood fats

Dysphagia - difficulty in swallowing

Dysphasia - difficulty in communicating

Dyspraxia - difficulty carrying out purposeful movement

Dystonia – muscle dysfunction characterised by spasms or abnormal muscle contraction

Echocardiogram - ultrasound test on heart function

Embolus - clot of blood in the bloodstream

Emotional liability - a condition where the mood of the person changes rapidly

Enteral feeding - feeding with use of a tube

Flaccidity - floppy muscles

Gait - how you walk

Haemorrhage - bleeding

Hemianopia - loss of half your field of vision in each eye

Hemiparesis - weakness in one side of the body

Hemiplegia - loss of movement in one side of the body

Hemisphere of the brain - one side of the brain

Hypertension - abnormally high blood pressure

Incontinence - loss of control over bladder or bowel functions

Infarction - area of dead tissue

Intravenous - in a vein

Involuntary action - one that the body does without you being aware

Ischaemia - the state of tissue when the blood supply has been cut off

Ischaemic stroke - caused when part of the brain has been starved of blood supply

Motor - movement

Motor nerve - nerve connected to muscle that carries messages from the brain

Oedema - swelling

Paraesthesia - abnormal skin sensations, possibly due to temporary damage to a peripheral nerve

Paralysis - loss of movement

Paraphasia - unintended words, phrases during speech

Paresis - muscle weakness

Perception - ability to receive and use information

Rehabilitation - help the disabled person reach their greatest possible independence

Sensory nerve - a nerve carrying information about heat, pain, etc., to the brain

Spasm - involuntary contraction of muscle

Spastic paralysis - loss of voluntary movement, but where muscles can act on their own

Spinal cord - hollow structure that carries the main motor and sensory nerves; it runs from the medulla in the skull to the lower back.

Stroke - sudden damage to nerve cells in the brain

Subarachnoid haemorrhage – sudden bleeding between the brain surface and one of the thin layers of tissue covering the brain

Thrombus - a clot formed within the heart or a blood vessel

Tone - the amount of tension in a muscle at rest

TIA (transient ischaemic attack) - a mini stroke symptoms that only last for 24 hours

Vascular - the blood supply

Voluntary movement - movement that takes place by intention, e.g. reaching for something

Whanau - the extended family